# Ski
# British Columbia

Heather Doughty

LONE
PINE

*The publisher:*
**Lone Pine Publishing**
206, 10426-81 Avenue
Edmonton, Alberta, Canada
T6E 1X5

Canadian Cataloguing in Publication Data
Doughty, Heather.
    Ski British Columbia


    ISBN 0-919433-94-4


    1. Skis and skiing—British Columbia—Guide-books.
2. Ski resorts—British Columbia—Guide-books.
3. British Columbia—Description and travel—1981-
—Guide-books.  I. Title.
GV854.8.C2D68 1991      917.1104'4      C91-091796-5


Cover design: Beata Kurpinski
Editorial: Elaine Butler, Lloyd Dick
Design and layout: Lloyd Dick
Printing: Kromar Printing Ltd., Winnipeg, Manitoba, Canada

The publisher gratefully acknowledges the assistance of the Federal Department of Communications, Alberta Culture and Multiculturalism, the
Canada Council, and the Alberta Foundation for the Arts in the produc-
tion of this book.

For Victor,
who makes all things possible.

# TABLE OF CONTENTS

## ACKNOWLEDGEMENTS

My thanks go out to all the helpful people at the ski areas who were so generous with their information and time. If more people skiied, the world would be a better place, and these guys proved it.

Thanks also to Lone Pine Publishing for giving me the opportunity to fulfill a dream.

# British Columbia
# Ski Areas

(133)  Page number where
       description is found

# Introduction

*The view is spectacular at Cypress Bowl on the Lower Mainland.*

Eons ago, the floor of the Pacific Ocean bumped into British Columbia. It was not a friendly meeting. The earth erupted into countless peaks and folds creating one of the great mountain systems of the world. Things have calmed down since then and Man, in all his ingenuity, has utilized some of the best of these mountains for — skiing. The ski lift carries us beyond the doldrums of valley life into the higher plane of endless glaciers, sparkling snow and crisp, clear air.

British Columbia is blessed with an abundance of just about everything: rain, snow, sunshine, strange politics, you name it. The constant Westerlies blowing in from the Pacific Ocean are the dominant factor in B.C.'s weather. Moisture-laden clouds bear down on the coast and enthusiastically deposit their contents on the mountain slopes. During the winter, all of this moisture means one thing — snow — and lots of it.

Ski season starts in mid-November to early December and, in some areas on the coast, lasts through April. Blackcomb Mountain even offers summer skiing on the Horstman Glacier. How does skiing in the morning and a round of golf in the afternoon sound? Many small towns in B.C. have developed their own ski hills, a luxury associated with Europe rather than right here at home, and while some of the names may be unfamiliar, each contributes its own unique stamp on skiing. Standing atop a mountain in British Columbia, about to descend on the first run of the day, is a moment to dream about. Peak after peak stretches away into the distance; the sun glints from the glaciers; and the air is brisk. Below, the runs have been groomed like a carpet and the mountain is yours. Heaven.

This book has been written as a biography of B.C.'s downhill ski areas. It goes beyond the nuts and bolts of how many lifts and hours of operation to let you in on tidbits of information that will give you a feel for the ski area, in short, its personality. A story is told of each area that will round out your knowledge, allowing you to make an informed decision about which ski area fits your needs. You will find out when the skiing is at its best, what type of clientele is catered to by the resort, the best runs, strengths and weaknesses of the hill and general information about the area's accommodation, restaurants and activities. There are many ski resorts in British Columbia from world-class to down home. One of them will offer the perfect ski vacation that you've always been looking for but didn't know where to find. Welcome to the British Columbia ski experience.

**OUT-OF-BOUNDS SKIING**

Before doing any out-of-bounds skiing at any of the hills, it is important to check with the ski hill about their rules. Some areas absolutely do not permit out-of-bounds skiing and will take away your lift ticket.

Any out-of-bounds skiing should only be done with a thorough knowledge and understanding of the hazards involved.

Heli-skiing in British Columbia is world-reknowned. Operations such as Canadian Mountain Holidays and Mike Wiegele offer the ultimate ski vacations. Its cousin, snow-cat skiing, originated in B.C. and is fast gaining a loyal and growing following. The common denominator between the two is a quest for the best powder and, with the guides' intimate knowledge of the mountains, they find it.

The guides and the rest of the staff of these operations are there because of their own love of powder skiing and their wish to share it with others. All guides are fully qualified and have passed stringent tests with knowledge gained by years spent in the mountains. They have an in-depth knowledge of the mountains they are skiing and of the snow pack experienced in the area. While avalanche forecasting is not perfect, these people are the best qualified to make the decisions of where and when to ski.

The Bugaboos, Selkirks and Purcell mountain ranges, the heart of heli- and cat-skiing operations in B.C., are acknowledged as the best powder skiing areas in the world. They receive overwhelming amounts of light, dry champagne snow that is every powder skier's ultimate dream. In the spring, the slopes are covered with corn snow, or "hero snow" as it's also called, making everyone ski like a pro or at least feel like one. To round out the experience, skiers are accommodated in rustic, yet fully

*Heli-skiing is popular in B.C.*

equipped lodges, often inaccessible by car, that further complete the feeling of "getting away from it all" and enhance the camaraderie among the guests. Many of the patrons of these outfits are repeat offenders who can't get enough of the thrill of endless peaks, endless runs and thigh-deep, blow-away snow. The shared excitement and adrenaline establishes a rapport between everyone involved that, for many, is as addictive as the skiing itself.

The most difficult thing about skiing in British Columbia is deciding where to go. I hope this book will make the choice easier and get you on your way to a fun and satisfying ski holiday.

# Vancouver Island

*Mount Washington provides a vast array of incredible views.*

Vancouver Island is known for its dramatic coastline, abundant rainfall and Victoria — B.C.'s picturesque capital. In winter, the abundant rainfall descends as heavy snowfalls in the mountainous interior and results in great ski conditions at the three Island areas. A scenic, one-and-a-half-hour ferry ride from Horseshoe Bay just north of Vancouver will carry you across to Nanaimo, leaving a quick drive up to the ski areas. Neighbouring Courtenay and Comox are home to Mount Washington and Forbidden Plateau, the two most well-known hills, while on the northern end of the island, Mt. Cain, near Port McNeill, provides great skiing for the lucky few in the neighbourhood.

# FORBIDDEN PLATEAU

Forbidden Plateau Recreation Ltd.
2050 Cliffe Avenue
Courtenay, B.C.
V9N 2L3

Information:(604) 334-4744
Snow Phone: (604)338-1919

**A** *Orange Chair*      **C** *Look-out T-bar*      **D** *Ski School Tow*

**B** *Slalom T-bar*

**How To Get There**: Forbidden Plateau is located 14 miles (8 miles paved, 6 miles gravel, maintained by the department of Highways) from downtown Courtenay. Accommodation is available in Courtenay.

With the Comox Glacier behind, the Strait of Georgia spread out in front and open sunny slopes at your feet - this is skiing at Forbidden Plateau. The philosophy of this ski hill is "Fun, Quality and Affordability," and they live up to the promise.

Forbidden Plateau was once a taboo spot visited only by the Native medicine men. But today, with the help of chairlifts and skis, this area can be visited and enjoyed by everyone. The resort is open year-round,

*The base lodge at Forbidden Plateau.*

and the ski season generally begins in mid-December and lasts until April. Keep in mind that Forbidden is only open Friday, Saturday, Sunday and school holidays.

Vancouver Island consistently receives the largest snowpack in Canada. The storms blowing in off the Pacific get dumped right on the mountains of the island and the ski hills benefit. Forbidden Plateau receives an average of twenty-five feet of snow each year.

The mountain is steeper on the top half and more gentle below. There are a wide variety of runs to ski, from the meandering J-Way at 2.5 km long to the Kandahar downhill run. Ride to the peak on the Orange chair and tackle the Face under the lift or the neighbouring runs, Upper Boston and Corkscrew. You'll be relieved when you cross the J-Way and things get easier. That is, of course, unless you go straight from Corkscrew to Boneshaker.

There are easier routes down the hill on Boston (not Upper Boston) or you could ski over to the Lookout lift on Little Dipper or Roller Coaster. The Lookout lift accesses a knob off to the side and is beginner/intermediate terrain.

A handle tow next to the lodge is a good spot for beginners and children. The Slalom lift at the base, beside the orange chair, is one step up and good for training. Forbidden's Kinderski program, for 3 to 10 year olds, teaches the young ones how to handle their skis in a fun and relaxed atmosphere. Kinderski includes supervision/lesson, ski rental and lifts. Classes for the younger ages are held for two hours in the morning and two hours in the afternoon. Special programs are arranged for handicapped persons.

The daylodge is a classic. It's that Canadian-European style with white stucco arches supporting a wide, gently sloping second storey with big windows to capture the view and lots of sunlight. There's more than enough room for everyone in this spacious lodge. Try the fresh baked goods.

Forbidden always seems to have some special event planned. The Vancouver Island Snowboard Competition is held in January, followed by a provincial Para-ski meet. The Outlaw Dual Slalom Drag Race in February shouldn't be missed, and for the little ones, the annual Kinderski Race and BBQ is a fun event. But it's the annual running of the Kandahar Downhill in March that brings notoriety to Forbidden. This race has been going on for over 40 years! The annual Winter Carnival is a great family event the first week in February. The Torchlight Parade kicks off the festivities, and the Giant Slalom Race held during the carnival is a major attraction.

The friendly atmosphere at Forbidden is noticeable. It's a family mountain that offers variety and admits it's just out to have fun. The view is spectacular; the snow is deep; the skiing is good; and the drive is a joy.

## FORBIDDEN PLATEAU

**Vertical**: 349 m/ 1,150 ft.

**Elevations**: Base  1,047 m/ 2,300 ft.
Top  1,396 m/ 3,450 ft.

| **Lifts**: | Vertical | Length |
|---|---|---|
| Orange Double Chair | 311 m/ 1,020 ft. | 1,371 m/ 4,500 ft. |
| Slalom T-bar | 98 m/ 320 ft. | 427 m/ 1,400 ft. |
| Look-out T-bar | 76 m/ 250 ft. | 548 m/ 1,800 ft. |
| Ski School Handle Tow | 18 m/ 60 ft. | 122 m/ 400 ft. |

**Lift Capacity**: 3,400 skiers per hour

**Terrain Breakdown**: 40% Beginner
50% Intermediate
10% Advanced

**Total Terrain**: 407 acres

**Average Snowfall**: 7.5 m/ 300 inches (25 ft.)

**Number of Runs**: 21

**Facilities**: Daylodge, cafeteria, licensed lounge, ski school, lockers and change area. Ski rentals (alpine, nordic & snowboard), sales and repairs are located in an adjacent building.

**Season Dates**: Mid-December to mid-April
Friday, Saturday, Sunday and all school holidays except Christmas Day

**Hours of Operation**: 9 a.m. to 4 p.m.

| **1989/90 Prices**: | All Day | Half Day |
|---|---|---|
| Adult | $20.00 | $15.00 |
| Youth 13-18 yrs. | $17.00 | $13.00 |
| (Student I.D. required) | | |
| Junior 7-12 years | $12.00 | $9.00 |
| Child 6 years & under | free | free |
| Seniors & Disabled | $10.00 | $7.50 |
| Single Ride Chairlift | $5.00 | |
| Day Pass Booklets | $108.00 | |
| (6 Tickets) | | |

# MT. CAIN

Mount Cain Alpine Park Society
Box 1225
Port McNeill, B.C.
V0N 2R0

Lodging & General Information: (604)956-3849
Snow Report: (604)956-3744
Ski School: (604)281-2244

**A** *T-bar*          **B** *T-bar*

**How To Get There**: Following a scenic 75 minute drive north of Campbell River along Highway 19, is the turn-off to Mt. Cain. The base is a 16 kilometre drive on a gravel road, chains are mandatory on the last 10 kilometres.

Mt. Cain is a ski hill that shouldn't be measured by the lifts it offers, but by its terrain. Formidable, snow covered twin peaks jut above open bowls, blending into forested slopes down to small Mistaken Lake and the daylodge. Surprisingly, Mt. Cain has the second highest vertical drop on Vancouver Island at 450 m (1500 ft.). Unfortunately, its location, one and a half hours from both Campbell River and Port McNeill, puts it a little out of the way for most skiers.

## MT. CAIN

| | |
|---|---|
| **Vertical:** | 460 m/ 1,500 ft. |
| **Elevations:** | Base 1,200 m/ 3,900 ft.<br>Peak 1,650 m/ 5,400 ft. |
| **Lifts:** | 2 T-bars<br>1 Beginner Handle Tow |
| **Terrain Breakdown:** | 25% Beginner<br>50% Intermediate<br>25% Advanced |
| **Average Temperature:** | -3°C |
| **Average Snowfall:** | 400 cm/13 ft. |
| **Runs:** | 16 |
| **Facilities:** | Daylodge, ski shop, ski rentals, cafeteria, lounge, ski school, hostel-style accommodation, nordic trails, RV parking |
| **Season Dates:** | December - April |
| **Hours of Operation:** | 9:30 to 3:30<br>Open weekends and school holidays |

| **1990/91 Prices** | Full Day | Half Day |
|---|---|---|
| Adult | $20.00 | $15.00 |
| Youth (13 - 16) | $16.00 | $11.75 |
| Child (6-12) | $7.50 | $5.25 |

The locals don't mind, though. The area is operated by the Mt. Cain Alpine Park Society and is open only on weekends and school holidays. That means when the lifts start up Saturday morning, all the new snow and great tree skiing will be fresh and waiting for the select few who have made the drive.

The two T-bars serve the area well. The first rises from the lodge to a point half way up the ridge line. The Back Alley scoots you across to the other T-bar which takes you to the edge of the open bowls, an area that never sees a grooming machine. These upper reaches are left alone so that powder skiers can enjoy the untouched snow and revel in the tree skiing on this side of the mountain. The bowls are out of bounds, but the odd set of tracks will still be seen when the powder is right. The beginners' handle tow is available for those people just learning how to ski.

There are approximately 20 km of marked nordic trails surrounding the base of the mountain. The majority of trails are intermediate and advanced because of the terrain. Backcountry gear (telemark skis) may

*Low key Mt. Cain is a great place to have fun while avoiding the crowds.*

be more suitable for some of the tracks. There are some easier loops around Mistaken Lake and at the base of the ski hill. A hut near Lunch Lake at the farthest point of the trails is open for use.

Accommodation at the hill is limited to a hostel-style building with use of the daylodge kitchen. This is roughing it. There aren't any showers or other niceties, but if you're with a group, it can be fun. Pre-booking is a must. Other accommodation is available in nearby Woss or Sayward.

Mt. Cain can't be called a destination resort, but with its friendly, low-key atmosphere, it's a fun place to ski.

# MT. WASHINGTON

Box 3069
Courtenay, B.C.
V9N 5N3

Information: (604) 338-1386
Snow Phone: (604)338-1515 (Comox Valley Ski Report)
(604)287-SNOW (Campbell River Ski Report)

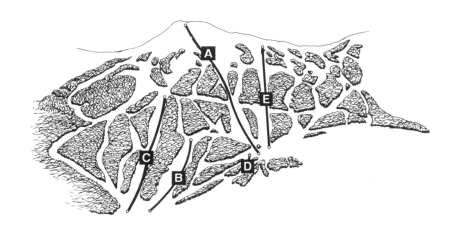

**A** *Blue Chair*  **C** *Red Chair*  **E** *Whiskey Jack Chair*

**B** *Green Chair*  **D** *Beginner Handle Tow*

**How To Get There**: Located above the Comox Valley just 45 minutes from downtown Courtenay. The last 18 km are on a well-maintained gravel road.

Mt. Washington is Vancouver Island's largest and most popular ski resort, attracting 260,000 skiers annually. It's also the only ski hill on the island that can be classed as a destination resort offering private on-mountain accommodation, an R.V. park, general store and extensive lodge facilities.

With a recent change in ownership, over a million dollars has been invested in the ski hill facilities. The largest undertaking has been a 14,000-square-foot expansion of the daylodge. A quiet apres-ski area downstairs complements the existing main bar, and a cappuccino and dessert bar will give you a pick-me-up after a hard day of skiing. In addition, a corner of the daylodge has been transformed into a fine dining room serving gourmet food. Mt. Washington is trying hard to provide the amenities and ambience that transform a ski day into a ski vacation.

The skiing is good at Mt. Washington — good but not great. They do get an amazing snowpack, 1,200 cm of snow each winter, but the proximity of the ocean doesn't often make for light, fluffy powder. The hill does have something for everybody so that all the skiers in the group can push themselves to their personal limits. Beginners should stick to the Green Chair, just downhill from the lodge. If you're a first time skier, a small beginner lift is located next to the lodge.

## MT. WASHINGTON — VANCOUVER'S BACKYARD

**By Car:**  The Comox Valley is 3 hours north of Victoria, and from the Lower Mainland, a 90-minute drive from Nanaimo following a 90-minute ferry ride from Horseshoe Bay, Vancouver.

**By Bus:**  *Vancouver Island Coach Lines:* (604) 388-5248
Leaves Victoria at 5 a.m. every Saturday and Sunday and most holidays. Mid-week runs also.
*Hilo Transport:* (604)334-2544
Daily pickup in four Comox Valley locations at 7:30 a.m. and return in afternoon.
*Victoria Ski Bus:* (604)381-SKIS
Departs Victoria Saturdays and Sundays at 5 a.m., arriving on Mt. Washington at 9 a.m. Departs at 4 p.m. and arrives in Victoria at 8:30 p.m. Breakfast & dinner stops in Nanaimo.

**By Sea:**  *B.C. Stena:*
Vancouver Island Princess
U.S. Phone 1-800-962-5984
B.C. and Alberta Phone 1-800-323-5984
Scheduled departures from Seattle at 10 a.m.; return trips from Victoria at 5:30 p.m.
*B.C. Ferries:*
Taped messages
Vancouver Phone (604)685-1021
Victoria Phone (604)656-0757
Nanaimo Phone (604)753-6626
Daily scheduled departures from Horseshoe Bay to Nanaimo at 7, 9, 11 a.m. and 1, 3, 5, 7 and 9 p.m.

**By Air:**  *Air B.C.*
For winter schedules, phone 1-800-663-0522
*Time Air*
For winter schedules, phone 1-800-663-3502

Intermediate skiers will find that most of the hill is made for them. The Red Chair, a short ski down from the lodge, services a large number of blue runs with a couple of black diamonds thrown in off to the right. More runs of this calibre are accessible by skiing from the Blue Chair and the Whiskey Jack Chair.

The area called Powderface, to the left of the Blue Chair at the top, is the obvious place to head for fresh snow. Steep pitches leading into Westerly and Tyee are quite fun, and the small bowl holds the snow in some good deep pockets among the trees. Watch out in this area for rock outcroppings. Powderface starts off nice and steep but all too soon flattens out into gentle cruising runs — the story of Mt. Washington. As the season progresses, make sure you get up the mountain early because the mild temperatures and sunshine can quickly turn the snow heavy and slushy.

Mt. Washington has a full offering of ski lessons and packages. A popular program for week-long visitors is the Adventure Ski Week: a 5-day holiday with daily guiding, lessons and dinner on Tuesday night. It's a good way to meet fellow skiers and improve your technique. A new program is the 50 Plus

*There's powder at the top, but it can turn to slush in a hurry in the spring sun.*

package that caters to active people 50 years and older at all levels of ski ability. As so many families head for Mt. Washington, they have three programs for kids up to twelve years old. The Kid's Brigade offers child minding for 2 to 4 years old in a large play area. It runs daily from 9 a.m. to 12 noon and another session from noon to 3 p.m. Drop-in child minding is offered anytime as long as the child is toilet trained. Kid's Skiing offers two hours of on-hill supervision and lessons for 3 to 7 year olds in morning and afternoon sessions. For the older kids, 5 to 12 years, the Hot Kids group is for the ones who can ski the more difficult runs and some of the most difficult runs. There are morning and afternoon groups as well as special camps throughout the winter.

Anyone who has ever been to Mt. Washington will tell you about the road up from Courtenay. It's a long winding gravel road that can be painfully slow if you get in behind a parade of cars and buses. Chains are mandatory in bad weather and can be bought or rented from Southeaster Snowchain, 338-1056, at the base of Mt. Washington.

Accommodation at the ski hill covers all needs. The alpine village provides private on-mountain chalets for families, couples and groups. The Mogul Home Park features full-service hook-ups and a recreation centre offering showers, washrooms, lockers, laundromat, games room, sauna and a social area. The park has an easy-access ski run and is within walking distance to the day lodge. Campbell's Mountain Hearth is a bed and breakfast offering home cooking, a hot tub, sauna and a warming wood-burning stove. Phone (604)338-4134. There are many more motels, hotels and bed and breakfasts in the Comox Valley. Phone the Chamber of Commerce (604)334-3234 or write them at 2040-A Cliffe Ave., Courtenay, B.C., V9N 2L3 for information.

Cross-country skiers will also have lots of ground to cover on Mt. Washington's 30 km of skating and double-track-set trails groomed by tiller-equipped snow cats. Beginners can head for the Lookout while intermediates can push themselves on the rolling terrain of Paradise Meadows and Jutland Trail. The West Meadow and the 12 km Lake Trail Loop will challenge the more advanced skiers. Lake Helen McKenzie, Battleship Lake, and the surrounding peaks of Strathcona Provincial Park create a spectacular backdrop.

Mt. Washington is Vancouver Island's favourite ski resort, but it's not content to coast on its reputation. The new management team is actively pursuing the expansion of the area into a first-class destination resort. This is already a good place to come with the family to enjoy the scenery and slopes and it will only get better.

# MT. WASHINGTON

**Vertical**: 478 m/ 1,600 ft.

**Elevations**: Base: 1,097 m/ 3,600 ft.
Top: 1,575 m/ 5,200 ft.

| Lifts: | Vertical | Length |
|---|---|---|
| Blue Chair (double) | 386 m/ 1,268 ft. | 1,408 m/ 4,620 ft. |
| Green Chair (double) | 140 m/ 342 ft. | 686 m/ 2,250 ft. |
| Red Chair (triple) | 215 m/ 701 ft. | 976 m/ 3,200 ft. |
| Beginner Handle Tow | | |
| Whiskey Jack (triple) | 290 m/ 952 ft. | 1,082 m/ 3,550 ft. |

**Lift Capacity**: 6,640 skiers per hour

**Terrain Breakdown**: 20% Beginner
50% Intermediate
30% Advanced

**Total Terrain**: 204 acres of cut runs, plus trees

**Average Temperature**: -1°C

**Average Snowfall**: 1,200 cm/ 472 in.

**Runs**: 25

**Facilities**: Nordic skiing, 2 daylodges, childcare, ski rentals, ski shop, 3 cafeteria/ restaurants, pub, ski school, accommodation, grocery store, liquor store, RV hookups.

**Season Dates**: December through April (weather permitting)

**Hours of Operation**: 9 a.m. - 3:30 p.m.

| 1990/91 Prices:* | Full Day | Half Day | 3 Day | 5 Day |
|---|---|---|---|---|
| Adult | $29 | $20 | $82 | $115 |
| Youth (13-18) | $26 | $18 | $75 | $102 |
| Child (7-12) | $18 | $12 | $50 | $71 |
| Seniors | $18 | $12 | $50 | $71 |
| 6 & Under | Free | | | |

| Cross Country Skiing: | 1 Day | 3 Day | 5 Day |
|---|---|---|---|
| Adult | $12 | $28 | $39 |
| Youth (13-18) | $12 | $28 | $39 |
| Child (7-12) | $9 | $22 | $29 |
| Seniors | $12 | $28 | $39 |
| 6 & Under | $9 | $22 | $29 |

* Special Monday - Friday Ski Week Packages available..Group rates available.

# Lower Mainland

*Spring skiing is just one of the benefits of the Lower Mainland's generous climate.*

The Lower Mainland is home to the bulk of B.C.'s population and to a wide variety of ski experiences. Vancouver skiers have the choice of three mountains operating only minutes from downtown: Grouse, Cypress and Seymour. These mountains are the first barrier that the snow-laden coastal storms meet, and before the storms can continue their journey, a lot of snow must fall. If temperatures co-operate over the winter, these ski areas can build up impressive snow bases and, while it's usually too wet to fall as powder snow, the skiing is good on soft, groomed runs. They are fun areas to ski with some challenging runs, and, with night skiing, where else can someone finish work at five and be skiing high above the city by 5:30?

# CYPRESS BOWL

Cypress Bowl Recreations Ltd.
P.O. Box 91252
West Vancouver, B.C.
V7V 3N9

Information: (604)926-5612
Snow Phone: (604)925-2704

## BLACK MOUNTAIN

**A** *Eagle Chair*

**How To Get There**: Watch for the Cypress turnoff on Highway 1 in West Vancouver. The snowbanks grow higher and higher as you wind up the 12 kilometre switchback road to Cypress Bowl. Occasionally, the tip of a sign peeks above the mounds of snow. Is West Vancouver really only 10 minutes away?

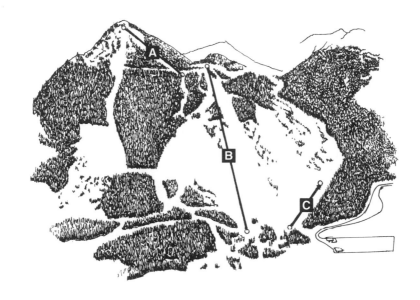

## STRACHAN MOUNTAIN

**A** *Sky Chair*        **B** *Sunrise Chair*        **C** *Easy-Rider Tow*

Cypress is a low-key gem. It has the longest vertical on the North Shore, night skiing, two lift-serviced mountains — Mt. Strachan and Black Mountain — a good variety of terrain and a fantastic view of Vancouver and Howe Sound. It also has some surprisingly good tree skiing on both mountains. It is quite popular with families from Vancouver and bus trips from the high schools which favour Wednesdays, Thursdays and Fridays. So come at the beginning of the week if you'd like to avoid the traffic.

Cypress seems to be in a time-lock, circa 1975. Except for the Sky Chair, nothing seems up to date or even permanent. It's actually kind of refreshing and funky. It has only been operating privately for 6 years; previously it was run by the Parks Branch which did very little in the way of upgrading facilities.

The two lift-serviced mountains at Cypress, Mt. Strachan and Black Mountain, have similar layouts. A chairlift up the middle, a beginner's trail looping around one side, an intermediate run around the other and then steeper chutes and trees down the centre.

Off to the right, at the base of Mt. Strachan, is a good beginner's area serviced by the Easy-Rider rope tow. There are actually two tows; one is adult height and the other lower for the shorter squads. Once you've mastered the rope tow and snow plowing, head up either the Sunrise Chair on Mt. Strachan or the Eagle Chair on Black Mountain. It's probably a good idea to avoid the Sky Chair and its expert terrain unless you have an extremely good sense of humour. Both mountains have easy runs to get you back down to the bottom. On Mt. Strachan, follow Collins and on Black Mountain, Panorama is the easy way out.

There are some fun glades to ski on both mountains. The right shoulder of Mt. Strachan and the area between Eagle Chair and Panorama are good areas to play around. These trees are within the hill boundaries and lead right back through open pitches to the chair lifts. It's a good idea to stay in bounds at Cypress because it's very easy to get lost and find yourself the topic of the six o'clock news.

Cypress Bowl turns into Cypress Beach in the spring. This phenomenon was begun by the skiers themselves and anyone else with a lawn chair and a pair of shorts. On sunny days the last two miles of the road are lined with sun worshippers sporting layers of Hawaiian Tropic and the latest in tacky beachwear. The ski hill followed their lead and each April, at the top of the Sky Chair, the management sets up a complimentary BBQ which attracts flocks of skiers and pink flamingos.

*Catch some rays during the long spring season at Cypress Bowl.*

## CYPRESS BOWL

**Vertical:** 520 m/ 1,700 ft.
Longest vertical on North Shore

**Elevations:** Base  930 m/ 3,050 ft.
Mt. Strachan  1,450 m/ 4,750 ft.
Black Mountain  1,200 m/ 4,000 ft.

| **Lifts:** | Mt. Strachan | Black Mountain |
| --- | --- | --- |
| | Sky Chair | Eagle Chair |
| | Sunrise Chair | |
| | Easy-Rider Tow | |

**Terrain Breakdown:** 45% Advanced
35% Intermediate
20% Beginner

**Average Temperature:** 1.5°C

**Average Snowfall:** 486 cm/ 16 ft.

**Runs:** 20

**Facilities:** Bobby's Lounge - licensed
Cypress Bowl Cafe - cafeteria located at base of mountains
Ski school, ski rentals, ski patrol, retail shop, lockers

**Season Dates:** December 1st to April 30th (weather permitting)

**Hours of Operation:**
All Day: 8:30 a.m. - 11:00 p.m. Weekdays
8:00 a.m. - 11:00 p.m. Weekends
Part Day: 8:30 or 8:00 a.m. - 12:30 p.m.
12:30 p.m. - 4:00 p.m.
4:00 - 11:00 p.m.
Night Skiing: 7:00 - 11:00 p.m.

| **1990/91 Prices:** | Full Day | Part Day | Night |
| --- | --- | --- | --- |
| Adult | $27 | $23 | $19 |
| Youth (13-18 yr) | $23 | $19 | $18 |
| Child (6-12 yr) | $14 | $10 | $10 |
| Scooters (5 under) | $1 | $1 | $1 |
| Seniors | $11 | $11 | $11 |

Cypress also offers a great deal on passes in the spring. At the end of February, $99 will buy you an unlimited pass for the rest of the season. It's worth it for the free burgers alone. The hill shuts down for the year sometime between April 30 and May 15, and with an average base of 300 cm, it's the lack of skiers rather than lack of snow that determines the end of the season.

Cypress Bowl is a good all-round hill for families and intermediate skiers because the terrain is varied and interesting. The hill is open until 11 p.m., and since it's only half an hour from downtown Vancouver, bring your skis to work and head up afterwards for a few turns. At least make sure you catch Cypress on those beautiful spring days when everyone is energized and working on an early tan. As they say, come on up and "Ski The Sky".

# GROUSE MOUNTAIN

6400 Nancy Greene Way
North Vancouver, B.C.
V7R 4K9

Information: (604)984-0661
Guest Services/ Ski School: (604)980-9311
Snow Phone/ Lesson Confirmation: (604)980-6262
Dinner Reservations: (604)986-6378

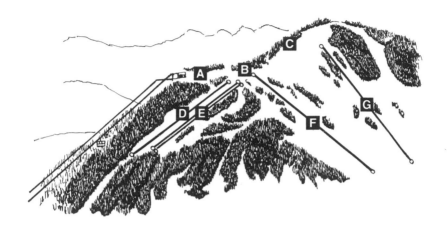

**A** *Peanut Bowl Rope Tow*   **D** *Cut Chair*   **F** *Blueberry Chair*
**B** *Paradise Rope Tow*   **E** *Cut T-Bars*   **G** *Inferno Chair*
**C** *Peak Chair*

**How To Get There:** Highway 1 - Coming from the east, follow Highway 1 until Capilano Road in North Vancouver. Turn right to Grouse Mountain parking lot.
Highway 99/ Downtown Vancouver - Signs will lead you from Lion's Gate Bridge to Marine Drive and up Capilano Road.

If you're looking for an after-work charge of fresh air and fun, Grouse Mountain is a great choice. You can be at the hill in just 15 minutes from downtown Vancouver and ski until 11 p.m. The SuperSkyride gondola whisks you from lush, green North Vancouver to the sparkling white top of Grouse Mountain with the lights of Vancouver and the ocean stretching into the distance. It's a spectacular panorama and an exciting atmosphere.

*Vancouver is just 15 minutes away.*

The SuperSkyride, completed in 1976, holds 100 people and travels at up to 33 feet per second, carrying you to 3,700 feet above sea level in only 4 minutes. That's a lot different than at the turn of the century, when it took all day to hike to the top of Grouse Mountain and only the strongest made it.

Grouse doesn't have a great deal of vertical, but it does have a good variety of terrain. The beginners have an area to themselves serviced by the Cut chairlift and T-bar. It's set at an angle to the rest of the mountain and avoids the main route of traffic.

The Inferno and Peak Chairs access the toughest runs on the mountain. With names like Hades, Purgatory and Inferno you know that you had better be on top of your skis or the consequences could be hellish. These narrow chutes drop sharply off the edge of the peak through massive snow-encrusted coastal mountain trees. The chutes open up halfway down to rolling terrain scattered with smaller trees and over to the Inferno Chair or the Blueberry Chair for the ride back to the main chalet.

The Grouse Ski School is one of Canada's largest and offers a different program for all levels of skiing. An interesting variation is the use of the SyberVision training technique. In a small theatre, students watch videos of expert skiers doing all the right moves. Slow motion, different viewing angles and repetition of sequences are shown to help the students absorb the movements so they can reproduce them on the hill.

The Freeway program for teens aged 13 to 18 is for advancing skiers who want to challenge bumps and gates with expert coaching. There is a choice of one- or four-day packages, and all clinics are three hours, 9 am. to 12 noon, weekends and holidays.

Action Snowboarding Camps will get you in on the latest craze in downhill motion. Grouse offers 4 night camps and 2 day/all day camps on the weekends. It includes four 2.5 hour sessions, top level coaching, video analysis, fun race and end of the day socials.

## GROUSE MOUNTAIN

**Vertical**: 365 m/ 1,200 ft.

**Elevations**: Peak of Grouse Mtn. 1,249 m/ 4,100 ft.
Base of SuperSkyride 289 m/ 950 ft.
Grouse Nest 1,138 m/ 3,700 ft.

**Lifts**: Peanut Bowl Rope Tow
Paradise Rope Tow
Peak Chairlift
Cut Chairlift
Cut T-bars
Blueberry Chairlift
Inferno Chairlift

**Lift Capacity**: 5,500 skiers per hour

**Terrain Breakdown**: 30% Beginner
50% Intermediate
20% Expert

**Runs**: 12 Runs - 8 open for night skiing

**Total Terrain**: 120 acres/ 49 hectares

**Average Temperature**: -2°C

**Average Snowfall**: 5 m/ 200 in. (with snowmaking)

**Facilities**: Main Chalet - Grouse Nest Restaurant,
Snack Bar,
Light Moala Bistro, nightly live entertainment,
Ski Check, ski school, race course

**Season Dates**: December 1st - Mid-April (weather permitting)

**Hours of Operation**: 8:30 a.m. - 11:00 p.m.

**Snowmaking**: 75% of area (All beginner terrain covered)

**Annual Events**: Spring Carnival
The Slush Cup
Heritage Classic Gelundesprung

| **1990/91 Prices** | Full | Part |
|---|---|---|
| Adult | $28.00 | $18.00 |
| Youth | $23.50 | $18.00 |
| Child | $13.00 | |
| 5 and under | FREE | |

Ski Grouse on Tuesday nights for race training at 7:30 p.m. as well as helpful hints from the coaching staff. You can also race against the clock on your own most weeknights and weekends. Call the Ski School for details at (604)980-9311. Buy a season's pass and automatically become a Club Grouse member or pick up the Club Grouse Discount card and ski for only $9.99 each time. With the discount card, skiing is free on Sunday nights for you and a friend, as is the ski check when you take a break in the Grouse Nest. The discount card is a great idea if you don't want to commit to buying a full season's pass but a lot of people find they have so much fun, they buy a pass the next year. Both passes are valid through the summer as well.

Grouse Mountain is a perfect outing for non-skiers, too. The Grouse Nest restaurant must have the best view in town with Vancouver spread out below like a twinkling tablecloth. The food in front of you is also very appealing. The pub next door serves up tasty bar food, including excellent nachos and cool pints, when you need a break from the great outdoors. After dinner, take a ride on a horse-drawn sleigh. It starts at the top of the Skyride and heads up toward Blueberry peak and then back in twenty minutes. The sleigh carries fifteen to twenty people and costs $6 for adults and $3 for children.

Grouse is a very social mountain. The skiing is fun and in the evenings, it feels like most people are going to a party. Excitement is high and the view is spectacular. With the hours that Grouse keeps, everyone should be able to fit it into their schedule. That really is the beauty of Grouse. It's only fifteen minutes from Vancouver, and it's a great place to spend a few hours having fun and meeting old and new friends.

# HEMLOCK

Box 7, Site 2, RR#1
Agassiz, B.C.
V0M 1A0

Information: (604)797-4411
Mountain Accommodation: (604)797-4444
Snowphone: (604)520-6222

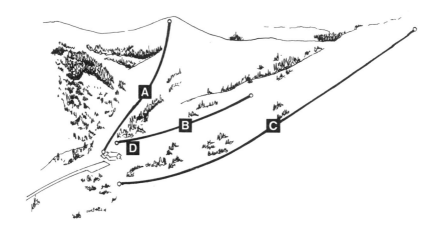

**A** *Skyline Chair*  **C** *Sasquatch Chair*  **D** *Strawline Handle Tow*
**B** *Whistlepunk Chair*

**How To Get There**: Follow either Hwy 1 or Hwy 7 east from Vancouver. Hwy 1 travellers must cross the Fraser River to Mission or, if coming from the east, cross to Agassiz. Follow Hwy 7 to Harrison Mills and turn north on Morris Valley Road. Watch for the "Welcome to Hemlock Valley" sign.

Hemlock is only one hour from Hope and Port Coquitlam and 120 km (75 miles) from Vancouver.

International Stage Lines - Ski bus pick up and return trip from Surrey, Langley, Aldergrove and Mission. (604)270-6135

When you arrive in the parking lot at Hemlock, ten to twelve foot snowbanks and a panoramic view of the ski hill greet you. The ski area is a logged ridge that forms a natural amphitheatre for the large amounts of snow this valley receives. Although it lacks challenging terrain, Hemlock is a good hill for families and weekend skiers who are looking for a low-key vacation and a community atmosphere.

Two chairlifts reach to the top of the ridge and provide access to the entire area. A road is groomed along the top, and you can ski along it from the chair and drop down virtually anywhere that looks interesting. While there are signs naming designated runs, the boundaries are indistinct as many, especially on the Skyline Chair side, have no trees dividing them and little grooming.

The triple Sasquatch Chair accesses a higher bump on the ridge and several intermediate paths such as Abominable, Bigfoot, Chehalis, Cheam and Weaver are groomed to the bottom. This could be considered the cruising area of the hill, and the Skyline Chair is the steeper side, offering more mogul runs.

The most challenging runs on the hill are found on the west side. Turning right off the Skyline Chair and zipping along the ridge, you can choose from The Happy Hookers (really!) and Outrigger for steeper, but fairly short pitches. These are not groomed and are fun on a powder day. The main face does get direct sunlight, so you want to start skiing early in the morning before the snow sets up.

Following the ridge in the opposite direction will offer you runs for all abilities. The beginner will want to continue on Slackline to the bottom. Timber Cruiser, to the right, is a little more difficult. A run called Heaven truly is for mogul skiers. All runs at the hill funnel down to the base lodge area and back to the lifts. Parents appreciate this feature because it's easy to keep an eye on the kids.

In the centre of the ski hill base area are two beginner lifts that only go part way up the hill and are closed off from through traffic. The Whistlepunk double chairlift provides 91 m of vertical and is the next challenge after the Strawline handle tow is mastered. A winding gully beside the two chairs is perfect for kids to play in and challenge themselves on its rolls and banks.

Hemlock has a ski program for all ages and abilities. Mini Sliders are kids aged three to six years, and there are two-hour daily lessons for them at either 10:30 a.m. or 1:30 p.m. The Junior Challenge is specially designed to coach youngsters aged seven to fifteen years. All skiing levels from novice to beginning racer are covered. There are drop-in lessons as well as weekly programs. Hemlock Ski School also organizes

## HEMLOCK

**Vertical:** 396 m/ 1,300 ft.

**Elevations:** Base 975 m/ 3,200 ft.
Top 1371 m/ 4,500 ft.

**Lifts:**
Skyline Double Chair 335 m/ 1,097 ft.
Whistlepunk Double 91 m/ 298 ft.
Sasquatch Triple 348 m/ 1,140 ft.
Strawline Handle Tow 22 m/ 72 ft.
**Lift Capacity:** 4,200 skiers per hour

**Terrain Breakdown:** 20% Beginner
60% Intermediate
20% Advanced

**Average Temperature:** -1 to -3°C

**Average Snowfall:** 500 - 700 cm/ 16-23 ft.

**Number of Runs:** 21

**Season Dates:** Mid-December to April (Easter)

**Hours of Operation:**
Thursday - Sunday 9:00 - 4:00 p.m.

**Facilities:** • Wee Care: 8 months & up $3.00/hr/child,
reservations required. Open 9 a.m. - 8:00
p.m.
• Wild Willie's Pub. serves bar food (burgers,
salads, finger food)
• Cafeteria, Ski School, Ski Rentals, outdoor
patio, accessory shop, BBQ, video games
room.
• Snowmaking for bottom area.

| 1990/91 Prices: | Full Day | Half Day |
| --- | --- | --- |
| Adult | $26 | $20 |
| Youth (13-17) | $23 | $18 |
| Child (7-12) | $14 | $18 |
| 6 & Under | FREE | |
| Seniors | $14 | $12 |
| Cross Country | $7 | |

*Hemlock is a great family ski destination.*

four day-camps throughout the season and during Christmas and Easter breaks. The Coca-Cola Family Classic brings families together in friendly competition with each other, every weekend. This parent and kid dual slalom race is held with the combined time posted against other families. It's always a good way to meet people.

Wee Care will look after the really little ones while you ski. They have their own building at the base and can accommodate children eight months and up. Reservations are required. They are open from 9 a.m. to 8 p.m. and charge a nominal fee.

The Hemlock ski village is spread across the valley. The European-style chalets nestle under the ridge and provide contrast to a modern three storey condominium complex on the other side. Most of the cabins are privately owned but a good number are rented. The 110 bedroom condotel has bachelor, one and two bedroom units with complete kitchen facilities and jacuzzis and saunas in each of the two buildings. All are within walking distance to the lifts. Call the Inn manager at (604)462-7927 (toll free from Vancouver) or (604)797-4444.

There are a few stipulations to staying in these facilities. There is a minimum two-night stay on weekends, and a four-night minimum over Christmas break. Children under twelve stay free when sharing with their parents. Sorry, no pets allowed. Also, Hemlock has limited laundry facilities, so bring your own bedding and towels.

You'll have to make your own entertainment in the evenings because there's not much in the way of night life except for Wild Willie's bar which is open all day and occasionally has live acts. Consider a cross-country ski outing or night skiing if you're in the mood for some more fresh air and exercise.

Cross-country trails wind through the ski village and are a good way of getting around. They are relatively easy but there are a few hills and a lookout point above Edelweiss Drive. More adventurous trails start from the top of the Skyline and Sasquatch Chairs. The views over the back of the bowl while following the 6.6 km Backcountry trail are very scenic and you can see all the way to Garibaldi peak near Squamish. Kicker's Loop (1.5 km), Telemark's Delight (1.8 km) and Competition Loop (2.5 km) are all accessed from the ridge.

Hemlock is a good family resort that offers safe, fun terrain for beginner and intermediate skiers. It also has that elusive quality that many people are looking for in their vacation spots — a sense of belonging to a community.

# MANNING PARK RESORT

Manning Park, B.C.
VOX 1R0

Information: (604)840-8822
Vancouver Snow Phone: (604)733-3586

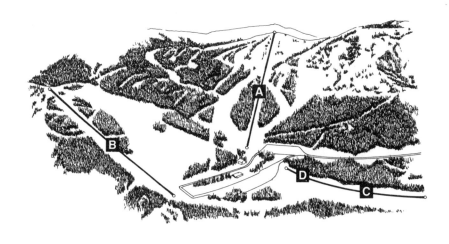

**A** *Orange Chair*       **C** *T-bar*       **D** *Handle Tow*
**B** *Blue Chair*

**How To Get There**: On Hwy 3, travel 209 km (130 miles) east of Vancouver or 177 km (110 miles) west of Penticton, B.C. There is regular Greyhound Bus service to the resort, six times daily.

The craggy, snow-swept peaks surrounding Manning Park ski hill are as impressive as the 6 m (19 ft.) of snow this area receives each winter. This well-rounded family resort is nestled in the heart of the rugged Cascade Mountains, only two and a half hours east of Vancouver. Manning Park Resort offers full resort facilities, including licensed child-minding and snowplay area, 30 km of cross country ski trails, serviced RV parking and a shuttle bus up to the Gibson Pass downhill ski area.

Manning Provincial Park, named for E.C. Manning, Chief Forester of British Columbia from 1935 to 1940, was established in 1941 and covers 66,500 hectares of rugged mountains and deep valleys. Two major rivers have their headwaters in the park: the Skagit, flowing west and south to the Pacific, and the Similkameen, which flows east to the Okanagan and is a main tributary of the Columbia. Miles of gravel roads and walking paths will get you into the heart of the park in the summer, and in winter, 30 km of the trails closer to the resort are maintained as cross-country ski trails while the rest are open for wilderness skiing.

The Manning Park Lodge, including the cabins and restaurant, provides the base area facilities. The ski hill is located 10 km back from the highway in Gibson Pass. The base facilities are the centre of operations with the ticket office, rentals, retail, ski school, day lodge and a complimentary shuttle bus to take resort guests up to the downhill area or to points along the cross-country ski trails. RV owners can take advantage of the extensive parking spots available to them, some with power, right at the ski area base.

Manning Park has a rather unique schedule of operations. On Saturdays, Sundays and holidays, all lifts are open. Thursdays, Fridays and Mondays are called Orange Days, when they only open the Orange chair and the handle tow. The ski hill is closed on Tuesdays and Wednesdays, except during Christmas holidays and March break. The cross country trails and accommodation are open seven days a week. Plan your vacation time carefully.

The hill itself is a weekend skier's paradise. Most of the runs are either beginner or intermediate, with one shoulder of the mountain offering some steeper, glade skiing for the stronger skier. The Orange double chair rises from behind the ticket office and drops you at the head of an array of runs. Off to the extreme right, the Horseshoe trail winds its gentle way down the mountain, connecting with the Fool Hen run and back to the bottom of the Orange chair. Off to the left is an assortment of intermediate pitches, or you can continue along the ridge to the black diamond area. This shoulder is the place to ski on big powder days as it gets lots of snow and is the best area to get enough momentum going to really be able to ski the powder. Many other runs, especially on the Blue chair, aren't that steep, and you can get bogged down.

Alternatively, the easier runs on the blue chair side are excellent for beginners and for skiers who enjoy gentle cruising. For kids and true beginners, a t-bar below the RV parking lot is a great place to learn. It's removed from the rest of the hill, and the gradual slope allows for concentration on ski technique without the worry of colliding with fast skiers. The snow play area for kids is also located on this side, just over from the top of the t-bar. A small rope tow is found here as well.

*On the slopes at Manning Park Resort.*

A variety of accommodation options are available at the base area. The Manning Park Lodge has 41 units with TVs, saunas, a games room and a conference room for up to 90 people. Every night at 7 p.m., movies are shown at the lodge for resort guests. Additionally, there are another 15 cabins and 4 chalets, all self-contained units with full kitchenettes, and the Last Resort, a group facility for up to 40 people.

The Pinewoods Restaurant is the only place for dining. A breakfast and lunch menu is served in the coffee shop during the day and dinner is served in the casual dining room from 5 p.m. nightly. A grocery store/ gift shop only stocks "convenience grocery and snack items," so bring food with you. Most of the ski packages include breakfast and dinner so you only have to provide for lunch unless you rent a unit with a kitchen and cook for yourself.

Windy Joe's pub is the skiers' gathering spot for a coffee beverage and game of darts. Bring your skates and the lodge will supply hockey or broomball nets for the night-lit skating rink at the base. So get a group together for a scrub match. If your muscles are aching after a hard day on the hill, slip into the Lodge saunas for a good dose of soothing heat.

Manning Park is a family resort that offers a good balance of terrain for skiers of all abilities. Couple that with the activities and reasonable accommodation packages at the resort, and you've got a fun vacation close to Vancouver but far enough away to feel like an adventure.

## MANNING PARK RESORT

**Vertical**: 432 m/ 1,417 ft.

**Elevations**: Base 1,357 m/ 4,451 ft.
Top 1,789 m/ 5,868 ft.

**Lifts**: Orange Double Chair
Blue Double Chair
T-Bar
Handle Rope Tow

**Terrain Breakdown**: 30% Beginner
40% Intermediate
30% Advanced

**Average Snowfall**: 576 cm/ 19 ft.

**Average Base**: 121 cm/ 4 ft. (December to April)

**Number of Runs**: 20

**Facilities**: Certified ski school, rentals, licensed daylodge, licensed child-minding, snowplay area, serviced RV parking, 30 km of cross country trails, full resort services within 10 km, complimentary shuttle bus to ski area.

**Season Dates**: Mid-November through early April, weather permitting

**Annual Events**: • Cascade Cup Spring Marathon (March): A 30 km cross-country ski event.
• Springfest Carnival (March): Fun for all ages with clowns, reasure hunts, BBQ and more.

**Hours of Operation:**

Tuesday/ Wednesday (except holidays) — Closed

Monday, Thursday, Friday — Orange Days (Orange Chair & Handle tow only - no half day rates)

Saturday, Sunday — All lifts

| 1990/91 Prices: | Full Day | Half Day | Orange Day |
|---|---|---|---|
| Adult | $23 | $16 | $14 |
| Youth (13-17) | $18 | $13 | $13 |
| Child (7-12) | $12 | $9 | $10 |
| 6 & Under | FREE | | |
| Seniors | $14 | $10 | $12 |

# SEYMOUR SKI COUNTRY

1700 Mt. Seymour Road
North Vancouver, B.C.
V7G 1L3

Information: (604)986-2261
Vancouver: (604)872-6616
Ski School Information: (604)986-2261
Snow Phone: (604)986-3444

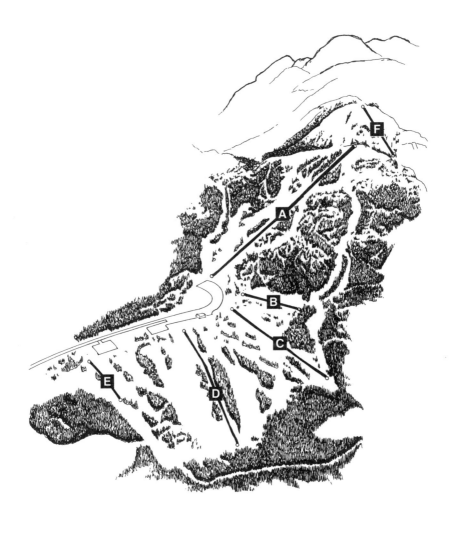

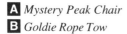 **A** *Mystery Peak Chair*
**B** *Goldie Rope Tow*

 **C** *Lodge Chair*
**D** *Ridge Chair*

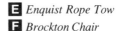 **E** *Enquist Rope Tow*
**F** *Brockton Chair*

**How To Get There**: In Vancouver, take Highway 1 (TransCanada) or Hastings Street to the Second Narrows Bridge (Cassiar Street). On the north side of the bridge, take thc third exit, Mt. Seymour Park, and follow signs east on the Mount Seymour Parkway. The Park entrance is on your left 5 minutes after leaving Highway 1.

Seymour Express Bus Route: The Seymour-CHRX AM600 Express first class coach has three routes running every weekend and holiday to most lower mainland communities throughout the winter. Call (604)986-2261 for information on this reserved pick-up service.

The view from the top of the Brockton Chairlift at Mt. Seymour is only the beginning of a long list of reasons to ski at this lower mainland mountain. Vancouver, Burrard Inlet, Indian Arm and the mountains surrounding Mt. Seymour Provincial Park provide such a breathtaking vista that you may forget you're only 22 km from the city centre.

Like the other lower mainland hills, Seymour emphasizes good times and good snow. With the highest base elevation of the North Shore ski areas,

*Seymour Ski Country.*

Seymour is likely to have snow even as sun bathers will be on the beaches below in Vancouver. None of these hills, Cypress, Grouse or Seymour, has a great deal of vertical elevation, but they are all good places for families, beginners and nine to fivers who want some fresh air and exercise after a day in the office.

The trail layout at Seymour is a little different from most areas and it works well in keeping the beginners and more advanced skiers out of each other's way. The Mystery Peak Chairlift rises from the parking lot and off to the side down the mountain from the road are two chairlifts and two rope tows. More confident skiers will head up the Mystery Peak chair and then either ski back down or cross over to the Brockton Chairlift which will carry you up to 1,400 m (4,600 ft.) above sea level. For the rest of the skiers, wide-open beginncr and intermediate slopes await off to the side of the hill; there's no need for a cold chair ride to get there.

Don't let this leave you thinking that you can only ski one area of the mountain. Both sides have a full variety of runs. The safest area for beginners and tots to ski is on the Goldie rope tow and the Lodge chairlift. These lifts only have green runs, and they're right out the back door of the lodge so parents can keep a close eye on their kids. The next one down, the Ridge chairlift, has some short intermediate runs and even a black diamond run, the Christmas Tree. Farther along, the Enquist rope tow services additional beginner runs, but pay attention because a black diamond run drops off below it. As with the other North Shore ski hills, don't go beyond the boundary where you run the risk of being lost on the lower reaches of the mountain.

On the uphill side, beginners can ski right from the top on Sammy's Run connecting with Manning although this area does have the highest concentration of higher level runs. The longest run can be made from the top of the Brockton Chair, continuing down challenging Unicorn and into Lower Unicorn to the bottom of the Lodge Chairlift. After that, it's probably a good time to go into the lodge and have some lunch. Make sure you try the treats from Seymour's very own bakery! The first-aid hut, ski school, cafeteria and ticket office are located along the outside edge of the curved main parking lot.

Seymour has been turning people into skiers for more than thirty years. With their new ski rental shop, now one of the largest in B.C., and more than 70 certified instructors, everyone can come up and give this great sport a try. Seymour Ski Country offers lessons for all abilities. Their Skiing is Believing course is a popular introduction to skiing, designed for people who have never skied before. The one-and-a-half-hour, one-time-only lesson is guaranteed to have you skiing, turning both ways and, very importantly, stopping. The package includes equipment rental, and a learners' tow lift ticket and must be pre-booked one day in advance. Another interesting group lesson is the Ladies Day/ Mums and Tots group lessons. The kids go their way and the moms go for their lesson knowing the kids are well looked after. Phone the ski school for more information on the rest of their packages.

Seymour has added a new dimension to their scene with a private meeting facility. Packages may include just the facility or be combined with skiing or guided snow shoeing outings. Seymour also offers their fun snow parties for groups of ten or more complete with lift tickets, use of the Labatt's Blue Ski Machine, ski video review and even pizza and beer.

Seymour, like all the North Shore ski areas, realizes that it doesn't have challenging terrain for advanced skiers so they specialize in providing a fun experience for families and beginning skiers. And within sight of downtown Vancouver, skiing doesn't get much more convenient for the urban dwellers.

## SEYMOUR SKI COUNTRY

**Vertical**: 366 m/ 1,200 ft.

**Elevations**: Base 1,034 m/ 3,393 ft.
Top 1,400 m/ 4,593 ft.

**Lifts**: Mystery Peak Chairlift
Goldie Rope Tow
Lodge Chairlift
Ridge Chairlift
Enquist Rope Tow
Brockton Chairlift

**Terrain Breakdown**: 40% Beginner
40% Intermediate
20% Advanced

**Average Temperature**: -2°C

**Average Snowfall**: 5.3 m/ 210 in.

**Number of Runs**: 25

**Facilities**: Rental shop-high performance demos,
snowboards and snowshoes, large snow
board half-pipe, ski shop, licensed cafeteria,
in-house bakery, brown bag room, lounge,
private meeting facility, private boardroom.

**Season Dates**: Late November through April

**Hours of Operation**: Monday to Friday 9 a.m. - 10 p.m.
Weekends/Holidays- Open 8 a.m.- 10 p.m.
Night Skiing 4 - 10 p.m.

**1990/91 Prices:**
Mon - Wed All Day* (9:00 a.m. - 4:00 p.m.) - $7
Full Day (9:00 a.m. - 10:00 p.m.) - $9
Thurs - Fri All Day - $11
Full Day - $13

Sat., Sun., and Holidays

|  | 8am-10pm | 8am-4pm | 1-4pm | 1-10pm | 4-10pm |
|---|---|---|---|---|---|
| Adult | $24 | $22 | $17 | $22 | $18 |
| Youth (13-17) | $20 | $18 | $15 | $18 | $17 |
| Child (6-12) | $13 | $11 | $11 | $11 | $10 |
| Child under 5 | FREE | | | | |

# Whistler

*The stark peaks of Blackcomb Mountain beckon skiers from around the world.*

A two hour drive north from Vancouver along beautiful Howe Sound and into the Coast Mountain Range brings skiers to world-class Whistler Resort. It is currently rated as the second most popular ski destination in North America and the number one destination for Japanese skiers. The reasons are numerous and obvious when you visit the area. The quaint, European-style village is nestled at the base of Whistler and Blackcomb Mountains, the two highest lift-serviced ski areas in North America. Each mountain has over 80 runs, an average of 1,100 cm (35 ft.) of snow each year, and a ski season that starts in mid-November and finishes up some time in April or May depending on the spring snowfalls. Blackcomb offers summer skiing in the high alpine from June to Labour Day week-end. The village also has a global array of restaurants and enough shops to make you tired just contemplating visiting them all. This is British Columbia's showpiece ski resort and attracts a world-wide clientele.

# WHISTLER RESORT

Whistler Resort Accommodation:
Vancouver Toll Free: (604)685-3650
Washington, Oregon, Idaho, Montana, toll free: 1-800-663-8668
Other Areas: (604)932-4222

*Blackcomb Mountain has become a challenger to Whistler's area dominance.*

**How To Get There: Follow** Highway 1 through Vancouver and take the Highway 99 turn-off at Horseshoe Bay. Whistler is 125 km (75 miles) north of Vancouver along spectacular Howe Sound and into the Coast Mountains (proper winter tires required).

Who would have known that Alta Lake would become a world class destination resort back in 1914? Not Alex and Myrtle Philip when they built the Rainbow Lodge for summer fishing excursions. They bought ten acres of lakefront property for $700. That's not enough money to pay for building permits in Whistler now.

The Philips, along with Myrtle's brother and father, took possession of the land in May, 1914 and began the huge task of clearing and construction. At the same time, the Pacific Great Eastern Railway was pushing its track through from Squamish to the interior and north. The train was a lifeline, carrying supplies and guests to the popular fishing resort for the three decades that the Philips kept their doors open. At its peak, the Rainbow Lodge was the most popular resort west of Jasper. It seems only natural that 75 years later, Whistler Resort would become one of the top recreation destinations in the world.

Many people remember the days of a narrow, winding gravel road to Whistler. Only the fanatics would make the harrowing five-hour trip to go skiing. The roads were plowed on Saturday mornings, so the Friday night drivers were in for an adventurous journey. If an oncoming car was met, someone had to pull over, quite often having to dig a nest in the snowbank for their car to allow room for the other to pass. Today, the Sea to Sky Highway is in the process of becoming 4 lanes from Vancouver to Whistler. This is only one of the many changes to the little community of Alta Lake.

The most remarkable transformation took place at the municipal landfill site. It is now Whistler Village. There is no hint of the site's past as you walk through the European style village today. It offers over 2,000 luxury hotel rooms and condominiums, and numerous restaurants, shops and nightclubs.

The village is designed for pedestrians. Park your car when you arrive and you won't need it again. A cohesive architectural style using wood and stone lends a cosy atmosphere to the town. Cobblestone walkways join the main village squares and the slow pace is the perfect antidote for jangling city nerves. A great day of skiing, an apres coffee drink, a soak in a hot tub - ahh, paradise.

Whistler has established itself internationally since its early days and is rated as the number one ski area with the Japanese and second by North American skiers. It's not only a fantastic winter destination though, because the summer activities are just as exciting. Hiking, windsurfing,

---

**WHISTLER – EASY ACCESS**

**by train:** B.C. Rail (984-5246)
*Daily service on one of the most scenic routes in Canada.*

**by bus:** Maverick Coach Lines - (604)255-1171
*Daily service from downtown Vancouver.*
Perimeter Transportation - (604)261-2299
*Connects between Vancouver Airport and Whistler.*

**Rentals:** Budget Rent-a-Car (604)932-1236
Avis Rent-a-Car (604)938-1331
Pacifica Limousine (604)731-0600

**Helicopter:** Canadian Helicopters (604)932-2070

*Blackcomb Mountain.*

mountain biking, golf, white water rafting, summer skiing and horseback riding are just a few of the recreational opportunities offered. Can you imagine your friends back home when you tell them you went skiing in the morning and played a round of golf on the Arnold Palmer-designed course in the afternoon?

It's difficult to keep up with all the changes in the valley. Initial development of the town centre proceeded in the late 1970s and early 1980s through financial ups and downs, but the biggest changes have taken place since 1986, when Intrawest Properties purchased a 50 per cent interest in Blackcomb Mountain and undertook the Blackcomb Benchlands development. The 330-unit Chateau Whistler, Canadian Pacific's largest hotel since the turn of the century, is the centrepiece of the area. In 1987, Blackcomb Skiing Enterprises put $26 million into mountain development including three high-speed detachable quad chairs: the Wizard, the Solar Coaster Express and the 7th Heaven Express, plus 2 T-bars on Horstman Glacier. In 1989, the Crystal Ridge Chair, a triple, and another high speed quad, the Jersey Cream Express, were added. The quads completely changed the nature of skiing in Whistler.

In the era of Blackcomb B.Q. (before quads), it took 45 minutes to get to the Rendezvous Restaurant from the valley. Now it takes 15, give or take 30 seconds, at full speed. That means, in a day you have an extra 2 hours on the snow rather than in the air. Oh, my aching quads!

Whistler followed suit in 1988 with a 10-person, high speed gondola from the town centre to the Roundhouse cutting their lift time on the north side of the mountain from over 1 hour to 18 minutes. The original gondola on the south side of Whistler is still running for those who have sentimental attachments to the old days of only a few years ago. The Green Chairs, serving a large beginner and intermediate area, were removed and replaced with a high speed quad chair that greatly improved circulation.

**Ski Esprit:** These mountains are so big that you will have a hard time finding all the different runs while on your holiday. The Ski Esprit Sightskiing program is a fun way to improve your skiing and explore both Whistler and Blackcomb with knowledgeable and qualified local ski instructors. They offer both a daily and four-day package that includes lots of extra fun perks. Phone the Ski Esprit Office, (604)932-3400 or Whistler Activity Centre, (604)932-2394 for reservations. Inquire at any Whistler or Blackcomb ski school location. Maximum group size is eight people.

Being located so close to the coast has its advantages: Whistler Resort is easily accessible, the temperatures are mild and they receive tons of snow. But all of these points can be looked at from the opposite side: the mountains are very crowded and those mild temperatures and snow can also mean rain in the valley.

Between Blackcomb and Whistler, you have two of the three highest lift-serviced mountains in North America and they are both on the expansion upswing. These hills can absorb a lot of people and keep them happy by offering countless runs and alpine bowls to explore. If crowds bother you and it's at all possible, try to avoid the classic busy times of the winter such as Christmas, March break, weekends and other holidays. Book your ski package for mid-week in January or February when the snow is dumping and most people are still recovering from their Christmas and New Year's blowout. Those two months are when the best snow falls and it's powder skier heaven.

As for the rain, don't let an ugly morning in the valley fool you. Nine point nine times out of ten, when it's raining in the valley, it's snowing like crazy in the alpine. Board the covered quads on Blackcomb or the gondola on Whistler to keep dry, and before you're past the first half-dozen lift towers, that rain has turned to snow - and lots of it. So while some people are moping around in the valley, you can be up on the mountain shredding the bumps and choking on face-shots. That's a lot more fun!

# BLACKCOMB MOUNTAIN

Blackcomb Skiing Enterprises Ltd.
4545 Blackcomb Way
P.O. Box 98
Whistler, B.C.
V0N 1B0

Information:Whistler (604) 932-3141
Vancouver (604) 687-1032
Snow report: Whistler (604) 932-4211
Vancouver (604) 687-7507

| | | |
|---|---|---|
| **A** *Wizard Express* | **F** *Cruiser Chair* | **J** *Crystal Ridge Chair* |
| **B** *Solar Coaster Express* | **G** *Magic Chair* | **K** *Glacier T-bar* |
| **C** *7th Heaven Express* | **H** *Stoker Chair* | **L** *Showcase T-bar* |
| **D** *Jersey Cream Express* | **I** *Catskinner Chair* | **M** *Wee Wiz Handle Tow* |
| **E** *Fitzsimmons Chair* | | |

Blackcomb has come a long way from its days as "Brand X", the new kid on the block trying to wrestle some of Whistler Mountain's long-time, loyal skiing population onto its fall line runs. Curiosity drew people over and the good, friendly service and great skiing kept them coming back. Since the high speed quad chairs were added and mountain expansions took place, Blackcomb has consistently drawn larger crowds of skiers to its slopes. Called the Mile High Mountain, it has the highest vertical gain in North America at 1,609 m (5,280 ft.). When you consider its thirteen lifts, four lodges, two lift-accessible glaciers and the endless combinations of its 86 runs, it's no wonder Blackcomb is considered a top ski destination around the world.

Blackcomb's base is located a short distance away from the town centre. The easiest way to get over there is to buy your ticket at the Carleton Lodge sales booth, ride up the Fitzsimmons Chair and then ski down to the base. Another option is to take a quick walk along the paved path through the woods to the main base. In the spring, Blackcomb has a shuttle bus that drives back and forth from the front of the day lodge to Whistler Village when skiing to the valley is no longer possible. If you're staying in the village, don't bother driving your car over and parking, it's just not worth it.

At Blackcomb, it's life in the fast lane. The Wizard and Solar Coaster high-speed quad chairs will whisk you from the Lodge at the base to the Rendezvous in fourteen minutes. The Wizard Chair carries you out of

*The distinctive rock outcropping at the summit makes Blackcomb's name a natural.*

the main base area to some lower runs perfect for intermediate cruising like Mainline and lower Cruiser. Snowmaking keeps these runs well-covered through the season. If the line-ups have already built up and you don't feel like standing around, board the Magic Chair, ride up to the Cruiser Chair and then hop onto the Stoker Chair. These are the original triple chairs and are slower than the quads, but by the time you stand in line it all evens out. At least you're moving. From the top of the Stoker Chair, you can access the Jersey Cream Express, the Solar Coaster, Catskinner Chair and the Crystal Ridge Chair.

The Solar Coaster Chair puts the longest fall line cruising runs in North America at your ski tips. Blackcomb built its reputation on trails like Cruiser, Springboard and Gandy Dancer, and with the high speed quads, you can ski more vertical than ever before. Offering a completely different pace, the challenging bumps of Catskinner and Gearjammer wait like land mines for the unwary skier or hero makers for mogul mashers. Zig Zag and Honeycomb lie in the middle of this ski spectrum, with their rolling transitions and perfectly groomed conditions, like a dream.

*Para-skiing at Blackcomb.*

Every chair is accessible from the top of the Solar Coaster. On busy weekends and holidays, it's a great idea to ski anywhere but this chair because it seems that most people will ride up and then ski directly back to it, causing massive line-ups. Check the light board beside the Rendezvous Lodge for approximate length of lines and, if you must ski back down this side, try riding back up Stoker Chair and over to Jersey Cream. Remember that Blackcomb is a big mountain. Take advantage of the choice of terrain and avoid standing in line-ups.

At lunch, stop in at the Rendezvous and choose from the cafeteria's make-your-own sandwich and salad bars, fresh baked pizza, Mexican and Italian food, burgers or soups and chilli. For the serious diner, and perhaps not so serious skier, Christine's is a full-service dining room that serves gourmet fare with a gourmet view. A comprehensive wine list complements the West Coast menu, and in the spring time, Christine's outdoor patio, North Beach, is the only place to have lunch. Try the South Beach patio for barbecued burgers and beer.

The Jersey Cream Express, another high-speed quad, follows the same route that old-time Blackcomb skiers will remember as Chair 6. Fortunately the lift line wasn't changed and if you're the exhibitionist type, a great run on a powder day down this uneven, rolling slash will still get the chairlift riders cheering. The beautiful, steep bump runs like the Bite, Staircase and the trees in between them are all just as exciting and formidable, and you can ski them more now that they are

*The South Beach patio.*

accessed by a quad. It also means you have to be there first thing on a powder day if you hope to have fresh tracks. There is no dawdling allowed on Blackcomb on those big deep days and among locals it's known as the Stress Machine. Go first, go fast or go home. This area is not reserved exclusively for advanced skiers though because there are great winding intermediate runs like Hooker, Cougarmilk and Wishbone.

The Crystal Ridge Chair is the newest area on Blackcomb. It used to be the secret trees and chutes of a favoured few, but now there is a whole network of intermediate trails slicing through the long ridge line. Good bump runs develop under the chair and, over the back, are some long cruising runs that take you around the shoulder of the mountain and back to the main face.

Seventh Heaven is the land of milk and honey on glorious, sunny powder days. South facing, blessed with incredible panoramas of endless peaks and glaciers, this face of the mountain has a mixture of wide-open bowl skiing in Xhiggy's (pronounced Ziggy's) Meadow, treeline glade skiing and long groomed trails like Cloud Nine and Southern Comfort. While some will be working on their turns, many will be working on their tans up on the deck of the Horstman Hut. This small log cabin at the top of the lift serves up licensed beverages, snacks, an incredible vegetable strudel and views that will have you scrambling for your camera. Don't leave home without it. That's Whistler directly to the south and Black Tusk, the cinder plug of an ancient volcano, is behind. The ragged glaciers of the Tantalus Range near Squamish mark the boundary of the world to the south.

Horstman Glacier is on the flip side of Seventh Heaven. It's an intermediate playground serviced by two t-bars. Afterwards, to head to other areas, ski along the Hot Rocks Traverse past the base of the Glacier T-bar over to Crystal Chair or out the bottom of the glacier back to the Jersey

*Rendezvous Lodge.*

Cream area along Bowling Alley, an intermediate roadway. Behind the Horstman Hut, is the entrance to the first double black diamond run in North America, the Saudan Couloir, the site of the annual ski race extreme in April.

From the top of Showcase T-bar is the access to Blackcomb Glacier, a wide open powder bowl that drops down onto a long traverse back to the bottom of Stoker Chair. The glacier itself is a safe mini-adventure for intermediate and advanced skiers. You have to hike up a bit to get to the entrance, pass by the steep half-pipe pitch of the Blowhole and out onto Blackcomb windrow, a long wave of snow formed by the glacier and the wind. The bowl rises up to a gently curving ridge where the occasional ski-tourer will be cutting zig zag tracks up the face to get to the deep powder of the pitches on the far side. Straight across from the top of the Blackcomb glacier is the long gash between the rocks called Husumi and to its left is the inviting powder shoulder of Corona. These areas are out-of-bounds and require the proper equipment and knowledge to ski safely. But if you're lucky, you'll see some wild powder hounds leaving billowing snow and perfect turns behind them down these faces. With that inspiration, push off the edge and dance down the glacier.

## BLACKCOMB MOUNTAIN

**Vertical:** 1,609 m/ 5,280 ft
**Elevation:** Top 2,284 m/ 7,494 ft
Base 675 m/ 2,214 ft

| Lifts: | Length | Vertical |
|---|---|---|
| Wizard Express (covered quad) | 2,230 m/ 7,316 ft. | 566 m/ 1,857 ft. |
| Solar Coaster Express (quad) | 1,931 m/ 6,335 ft. | 623 m/ 2,044 ft. |
| 7th Heaven Express (quad) | 1,790 m/ 5,873 ft. | 589 m/ 1,932 ft. |
| Jersey Cream Express (quad) | 1,551 m/ 5,089 ft. | 385 m/ 1,263 ft. |
| Fitzsimmons Chair (triple) | 822 m/ 2,930 ft. | 100 m/ 331 ft. |
| Cruiser Chair (triple) | 1,440 m/ 4,723 ft. | 388 m/ 1,275 ft. |
| Magic Chair (beginners double) | 646 m/ 2,119 ft. | 94 m/310 ft. |
| Stoker Chair (triple) | 1,563 m/ 5,130 ft. | 496 m/ 1,676 ft. |
| Catskinner Chair (triple) | 1,375 m/4,520 ft. | 363 m/ 1,192 ft. |
| Crystal Ridge Chair (triple) | 1,100 m/ 3,608 ft. | 360 m/ 1,181 ft. |
| Glacier T-Bar | 710 m/ 2,329 ft. | 205 m/ 673 ft. |
| Showcase T-Bar | 710 m/ 2,329 ft. | 205 m/ 673 ft. |
| Wee Wiz Handle Tow | 60 m/ 197 ft. | |

**Lift Capacity:** 23,860 skiers per hour

**Terrain Breakdown:** 25% Expert
55% Intermediate
20% Beginner

**Total Terrain:** 1,500 acres

**Average Temperature:** -4°C

**Average Snowfall:** 1,100 cm/ 35 ft.

**Runs:** 86

| Lodges: | Elevation | Seats |
|---|---|---|
| The Lodge (Base) | 683.5 m | 450 |
| Rendezvous | 1,860 m | 1,000 |
| Horstman Hut | 2,250 m | 40 |
| Crystal Hut | 1,800 m | 50 |

## BLACKCOMB MOUNTAIN - CONTINUED

**Facilities**: Kids' Kamp, ski school, Masters racing camps, ski & sport shop, rentals, repairs, valet parking, ski machine, guided tours, Video Memories, Mountain Mardigras (hosted, group, on-mountain picnic & ski day), Blackcomb Therapy Centre (physiotherapy, massage therapy, sun tanning salon)

**Season Dates**:

Winter: Mid-November to early May (weekends prior, weather permitting)

Summer: Skiing starts mid-June (weather permitting)

**Hours of Operation**: 9:00 am - 3:00 pm weekdays
8:30 am - 3:00 pm weekends
Mid-winter - lifts open until 3:30 pm

| 1990/91 Prices: | Full Day | Half Day | Whistler/Blackcomb combined pass |
|---|---|---|---|
| Adult | $40.50 | $33.00 | $42.80 |
| Youth (13-18) | $32.00 | $28.75 | $37.45 |
| Child (7-12) | $18.00 | | $20.30 |
| 6 & Under | FREE (must wear special ticket) | | |
| Seniors | $15.00 | | |

The snowboarders have adopted the windrow as their own massive half pipe. The wave of snow rises off the top of the glacier, crests and then rises up another eighty feet. On sunny days, the boarders hang out here, hiking up to the top pitch and riding down, performing radical tricks on the roll.

If you're a little intimidated by this huge mountain or just feel like brushing up on your technique a bit, Blackcomb has one of the most comprehensive ski-school programs around with the usual lesson packages. In addition. there are the Excel Programs, which were developed to help intermediate to advanced skiers bring themselves up to new levels. Consider the two-day ladies program, adult mogul camps, the Perception Ski Workshops and other Excel programs. Advance registration is recommended for all programs other than classes where daily drop-in is available. In Vancouver, call (604)687-1032. In Whistler, call (604)932-3141 or stop by one of their sales locations.

While you're out on the hill improving your technique, what about the kids? Blackcomb has been known for its innovative and fun instruction since they opened in 1980 and have been so successful that they had to double the size of the Kids' Kamp building and facilities. Larger registration, rental and eating areas all help to ease the way to a fun day of skiing. The Magic Chair behind the building is in the perfect location for beginners, offering an easy slope, slow-moving double chair and easy access to the day lodge. Wizard's World is a fun ski playground on Jersey Cream with machine-made rolling terrain for intermediate to expert skiers.

Blackcomb also offers organized three- and four-day ski weeks for children ages four to thirteen who are at least of the Red Riders level, which means they can turn both ways and stop. Included in the programs are a Monday Morning Family Breakfast at Johnny Jupiter's, awards, race and the Pepsi Kids' Night Out with jugglers, children's theatre and movies. Enjoy your own night out knowing the kids are all right. Registration can be done by mail, phone or in person at the Kids' Kamp Centre. There are some rules and regulations for registration. Be prepared for the crowds and allow 20 minutes for registration on the first day.

Blackcomb Mountain has grown rapidly in its first decade and has expanded its boundaries and horizons. It provides a first-class skiing experience, good, friendly service and more terrain than can be skiied the first time around. Whatever experience you're looking for, Blackcomb's got it. Steep and deep, gentle and safe, powder, sunshine - everything. There are a lot of ski hills out there, but not many mountains. Blackcomb is definitely a mountain.

# WHISTLER MOUNTAIN

Whistler Mountain Ski Corporation
Box 67
Whistler, B.C.
V0N 1B0

Information: (604)932-3434
Vancouver Toll Free: 1-800-685-1007
Snowphone: (604) 932-4191
(604) 687-6761

| | | |
|---|---|---|
| **A** *Whistler Express* | **F** *Scampland Tow* | **K** *Black Chair* |
| **B** *Peak Chair* | **G** *Scampland Tow* | **L** *Orange Chair* |
| **C** *Alpine T-bar One* | **H** *Green Chair Express* | **M** *Olympic Chair* |
| **D** *Alpine T-bar Two* | **I** *Big Red Chair* | **N** *Gondola* |
| **E** *Blue Chair* | **J** *Little Red Chair* | **O** *Olive Chair* |

Whistler is a mountain of surprises. Just when you think you've skiied all the runs, you'll discover a new area to explore. Whistler is also a mountain of variety. It's a giant of a ski hill where you can enjoy any type of experience you wish - cruise all day, explore the spacious alpine bowls or ski the huge silent coastal trees in powder up to your waist.

Whistler Mountain is the third highest lift-serviced area in North America and, with Blackcomb next door, Whistler Resort is heaven for skiers. The winter season starts early in the Coast Mountains as the first snow shows on the peaks in October, and the ski hills open in mid-November. Winter lingers in the spring, too, and the lifts

*Whistler Mountain.*

can run until mid-May. You have a long season to come out and ski, but try to avoid weekends and holidays because the hills become insanely busy.

Whistler's showpiece lift, the Express Gondola, holds 10 people per car and whisks you up from the town centre to the Roundhouse restaurant level at 1,840 m (6,000 ft.) in 18 minutes. The top terminals of the Express Gondola, Little Red Chair, Blue Chair, Green Chair and Big Red Chair, all meet here in a hub with the lifts and runs fanning out like the spokes on a wheel. To the south, you'll see Whistler Glacier, where the Peak Chair and the two alpine t-bars are located.

Whistler is known for its powder skiing and the best is found in the many bowls above treeline. This mountain gets 1,100 cm (35 ft.) of snow each year, most of it in late January and February. There's nothing like standing at the top of Whistler looking across endless glaciers and bottomless powder ready to push off for your next run. The Peak Chair will get you to the top of the mountain, and the two adjacent Alpine t-bars will scoot you up to the shoulder of Little Whistler and over into Harmony Bowl or into Whistler Bowl. These areas are not beginner slopes. There is a mid-station on the Peak Chair where you can off load, but make sure you know your limits because there are some extremely difficult chutes up there. At the top of the Peak Chair, a groomed road

*Whistler Mountain normally gets 35 feet of snow per year.*

off to the left will lead you along the top ridge lines of Whistler Glacier, Harmony Bowl and Burnt Stew Basin for wide-open, powder skiing.

Avid bump skiers will quickly head to the Blue chair area on the north side of the mountain. Here you'll find challenging runs like Dad's to the right and Chunky's under the chairlift. This is a great place to discover the thrill of victory and the agony of defeat — all to a chorus of cheers from the chairlift.

The Green Chair Express, a new high speed quad, replaces the two double chairs which serviced this beginner/intermediate area for years. For beginning skiers, the Green Chair area, along with Little Red, has a wide array of green and blue runs that will keep the excitement high and the fun factor going. From the bottom of the Green Chair, you can also ski down to the Black Chair which accesses a slightly higher level of runs and carries you back over to the Green, Little Red and the top of Orange chairs.

The Scampland Handle Tows for the kids are located at the mid-station point of the Whistler Express gondola. This area is wide open and protected from the main traffic flow. The Olympic Chair is right beside this area for the more advanced kids to try out. Whistler has many qualified instructors for all abilities and a number of special programs are available. For adults, try one of Stephanie Sloan's Women Only Ski Programs with an eye to developing ability and confidence in a relaxed atmosphere or, for the more intense, a Peak Performance Clinic.

## WHISTLER MOUNTAIN

**Vertical**: 1,530 m/ 5,020 ft.

**Elevations**: Base 652 m/ 2,140 ft.
Top 2,182 m/ 7,160 ft.

| Lifts: | Length | Vertical |
|---|---|---|
| Whistler Express | 5,012 m/ 16,444 ft. | 1,157 m/ 3,796 ft. |
| (10 people/gondola) | | |
| Peak Chair | 1,019 m/ 3,343 ft. | 401 m/ 1,316 ft. |
| (triple) | | |
| Alpine T-bar One | 926 m/ 3,038 ft. | 230 m/ 755 ft. |
| Alpine T-bar Two | 762 m/ 2,500 ft. | 200 m/ 656 ft. |
| Blue Chair | 914 m/ 2,999 ft. | 262 m/ 860 ft. |
| (double) | | |
| Scampland Handle | 117m/ 384 ft. | 22 m/ 72 ft. |
| Tows | 150 m/ 492 ft. | 35 m/ 115 ft. |
| Green Chair Express | 1,833 m/ 6,014 ft. | 424 m/ 1,391 ft. |
| (quad) | | |
| Big Red Chair | 2,345 m/ 7,694 ft. | 534 m/1,752 ft. |
| (double) | | |
| Little Red Chair | 1,237 m/ 4,058 ft. | 268 m/ 879 ft. |
| (double) | | |
| Black Chair | 1,717 m/ 5,633 ft. | 542 m/ 1,778 ft. |
| (triple) | | |
| Orange Chair | 1,238 m/ 4,062 ft. | 386 m/ 1,266 ft. |
| (double) | | |
| Olympic Chair | 769 m/ 2,523 ft. | 123 m/ 404 ft. |
| (triple) | | |
| Olympic Handle Tow | 250 m/ 820 ft. | 58 m/ 190 ft. |
| Gondola | 2,118 m/ 6,949 ft. | 640 m/ 2,100 ft. |
| (four people/gondola) | | |
| Olive Chair | 2,124 m/ 6,969 ft. | 649 m/ 2,129 ft. |
| (double) | | |

**Terrain Breakdown**: 25% Beginner
55% Intermediate
20% Advanced

**Total Terrain**:
Trails 275 hectares/ 680 acres
Bowls 610 hectares/ 1,508 acres
Total 885 hectares/ 2,188 acres

**Average Temperature**: -4°C

**Average Snowfall**: 1100 cm/35 ft.

**Number of Runs**: 90+

**Facilities**: Children and adult ski school, ski shop, ski
rentals, 2 bars, 4 snack bars, 3 restaurants,
2 ski machines.

## WHISTLER MOUNTAIN - CONTINUED

**Season Dates**: mid-November to end of April

**Hours of Operation**:
Until early February: Midweek 9:00 a.m. to 3:00 p.m.
Weekends 8:30 a.m. to 3:00 p.m.
Spring Hours: Midweek 9:00 a.m. to 3:30 p.m.
Weekends 8:30 a.m. to 3:30 p.m.
Mid- to end of season, via the Whistler Express gondola only.

**Annual Events**:
February: Peak to Valley Race
March: Fantastic Downhill
April: Masters National Alpine Championships
Mouton Cadet Spring Festival

| **1990/91 Prices\***: | Full Day | Half Day |
|---|---|---|
| Adult | $38 | $30 |
| Youth (13-18) | $30 | $25 |
| Child (6-12) | $16 | $13 |
| Senior | $30 | $25 |
| 6 & Under | FREE | |

*Sightseeing rate available on the enclosed Whistler Express Gondola.*

The Labatt's Blue Ski Machine at the top of Orange Chair is always ready for a dual slalom race on the same challenging run as the start of the Whistler Downhill course.

When you're staying in the village, it's easy to forget the base area at Whistler Creek on the south side of the mountain. This base was opened in 1966 and still operates a ski shop, cafeteria, pub and restaurant. The original 4-person gondola and double olive chair are open and if you're early enough, you can beat the rush by using these lifts. One of the great cruising experiences on the mountain is to ski down the Gondola run, part of the Downhill course, when it's freshly groomed, smooth and hard. A shuttle bus makes the run between both Whistler base areas.

A drawback to Whistler, though, is its lift system. Known as the Time Machine by locals, you enter in the 1990s on the high-speed gondola and spend the rest of the day in the 1960s riding outdated chairs and T-bars. It can be a frustrating day of line-ups and breakdowns. Even though Whistler had fifteen years to establish itself, it took Blackcomb just a few seasons to attract the bulk of the skier population over to its slopes. Now you'll find them there, jockeying for position on the high-speed quads,

on the runs, and for a seat in the cafeteria. These days, except for weekends, Whistler's slopes are relatively quiet with more room to move. Its
disadvantage has turned into a slight advantage for skiers if not for
mountain management.

In the spring, things really heat up at the Roundhouse and Pika's, the
two restaurants located next to each other at the top of the mountain.
Serving good food throughout the season, the spring sunshine brings the
BBQs out of storage, and it's mountaintop burgers and beer. Almost
every weekend there is an event or race of some sort and invariably,
everyone ends up back at the Roundhouse celebrating. Sun worshippers
crowd the rooftop patios and a party atmosphere reigns.

Whistler Mountain is a great ski experience. It's size, variety and
terrain offer endless skiing combinations, and when the snow really falls
in January and February, the alpine is a vast powder playground. When
you consider the world-class amenities of the resort village and the equally
incredible skiing on neighbouring Blackcomb Mountain, a ski holiday at
Whistler is a must on every skier's wish list.

# Okanagan Valley

*Weary skiers enjoy a soak in a hot tub at Cedar Hot Springs, near Silver Star.*

The famous sunny Okanagan Valley, a year-round playground, is now even closer to the coast. The Coquihalla Highway has cut the drive to the Okanagan resorts — Apex Alpine, Big White and Silver Star — to only three and a half hours from Vancouver. The resorts are busy planning new facilities and upgrading the old ones to accommodate the influx of skiers. Although they are busier than ever, there is still lots of room on the hills and in the resort villages. Best of all, they have retained their friendly atmospheres and enthusiasm about skiing.

Spring skiing in the Okanagan is an annual pilgrimage for many sun-seeking skiers around the province. The temperatures are mild; the sun is warm; and the snow is great, so everyone gets out and has a good time. If you're looking for a fun, affordable spring ski vacation, the Okanagan resorts are the places to be.

# APEX ALPINE

275 Rosetown Ave.
Penticton, B.C.
V2A 3J3
Okanagan Reservations:
Box 717
Penticton, B.C.
V2A 6P1

Adm. Office: (604)492-2880
Mountain: (604)292-8222
Snow Phone: (604)493-3606
Toll-free B.C., Alberta, Washington:1-800-663-1900 or
(604)493-3200

| **A** Stocks Chair | **C** Mill Chair | **D** T-bar |
| --- | --- | --- |
| **B** Novice Lift | | |

**How To Get There**: Located only 33 km (20 miles) west of Penticton off Hwy 97 on Green Mountain Road. A shuttle is available from Penticton to Apex Alpine 7 days a week. Greyhound Lines of Canada offers daily bus service to Penticton from all major centres. Canadian Airlines, Time Air and Air B.C. land at the nearby airport.

Steep chutes, long cruising runs and a wide-open beginner's slope are all on the menu at Apex Alpine. Of the three Okanagan resorts, it offers the most exciting and well-rounded skiing opportunities, along with the facilities and activities to create a good family vacation experience.

Apex offers a full service resort with restaurants, lodging, grocery and liquor stores, hot tubs, kids centre and an ice rink. An expansion plan will gradually add more amenities to the village. For now, they are a little short on accommodation at the hill although there are overnight R.V. lots available. The Dividend Lodge, named after a nearby peak, opened for the 1990/91 season and relieves some of the pressure for beds. If you can't get accommodation at the resort, there are a number of inexpensive motels by the lake in Penticton.

The skiing at Apex has always been good. Extensive summer grooming projects were undertaken in the late

*Welcome to Apex Alpine.*

1980s resulting in better snow coverage, wider runs and new runs. The Stocks Chair services a large intermediate cruising area, and a number of these runs were improved. The Whipsaw Trail, Whipsaw Run, the Old Mill Run and the easy out from the Ridge Run have all been widened to allow for better grooming, easier cruising and improved beginner terrain.

The Mill Chair extends to the top of the ridge and provides access to some really interesting skiing. Take off to the right and head for all the black diamond runs that come out above the Gunbarrel Saloon, the original daylodge. These chutes (K, Gun Barrel, Easy Rider and the rest) are all narrow pitches down through the trees that are exceptional on powder days. On the other side of the chair are the Bowls above the Stocks chair and Westbank, which both offer exciting skiing down steep pitches and trees.

The beginners in the crowd have two good areas to ski, the T-bar and the Novice lift. The T-bar runs up in front of the daylodge and has the big, wide Okanagan run for the descent. The public race course is on the other side of the slope. The novice lift is a gentle pitch down from the village that no one else skis on but the beginners. Nice and safe.

There is always something organized at Apex to increase the fun quotient. Welcoming receptions, ski movies, face painting, casino nights, and murder mystery dinner theatres are only a fraction of the activities available to guests. The Gunbarrel hot tubs are always in demand and are open from 3 p.m. to 9 p.m. Reserve by calling (604)292-8515.

Cross country skiers will find lots of trails to keep them busy. Twelve kilometres of trails were added which start and finish right in the village. They run along the valley at the base of the mountain and offer some scenic viewpoints of the alpine skiing, Beaconsfield and Apex Mountains. The 30-foot-wide trails are groomed with a twelve-foot flat section in the middle with set tracks on either side to allow for skating as well as classical cross country skiing. A small loop in the village is lit for night skiing and night-time activities.

The Nickel Plate cross country trails are about five km past Apex Alpine on the main road towards Nickel Plate mine. The club was formed in 1989 and has special programs and events to increase fitness and fun through cross country skiing. There are twelve kilometres of groomed track-set trails suitable for both styles of skiing. There is parking for up to 100 cars, solar-heated outhouses, and a 1,000-square-foot log home overlooking the meadows and Apex Mountains.

Apex Alpine is a versatile resort that offers a complete vacation for families. They also have some of the best ski terrain of the smaller destination resorts. If the future goes well for Apex, its expansion plans should only make a good resort better.

## APEX ALPINE

**Vertical**: 615 m/ 2,000 ft.

**Elevations**: Base 1,615 m/ 5,250 ft.
Top 2,230 m/ 7,250 ft.

| **Lifts**: | Vertical | Length |
|---|---|---|
| Stocks Chair | 300 m/ 1,000 ft. | 1,340 m/ 4,400 ft. |
| Mill Chair | 488 m/ 1,600 ft. | 1,465 m/ 4,800 ft. |
| T-Bar | 237 m/ 800 ft. | 844 m/ 2,800 ft. |
| Novice Lift | 47 m/ 154 ft. | 280 m/ 920 ft. |

**Terrain Breakdown**: 12% Beginner
50% Intermediate
38% Advanced

**Total Terrain**: Runs - 300 acres
Bowls - 15 acres

**Number of Runs**: 36

**Average Temperature**: -4° C

**Average Base**: 200-250 cm/ 6.5-8 ft.

**Facilities**: Ski School, Ski Patrol, Condominiums, hot tubs, ski shop, ski rentals, cafeteria, lounge, restaurants, bar, grocery store, liquor store, coin laundry, kids centre, sleigh rides, ice rink, RV lots, underground and day parking.

**Season Dates**: Skiing: December to mid-April
Resort: open year-round

**Hours of Operation**: 9 a.m. - 3:30 p.m. daily
Hours extended in the spring
Night skiing on Poma lift

**Nordic Skiing**: Apex Alpine "Village Central", 12 km of groomed and track set, additional 39 km at nearby Nickelplate Lake.

| **1990/91 Prices** | Full Day | Half Day |
|---|---|---|
| Adult | $29 | $21 |
| Youth (13-17) | $24 | $18 |
| Junior (9-12) | $19 | $13 |
| Child (6-8) | $13 | $9 |
| Seniors | $19 | $13 |
| Night Skiing: | Saturday 6 p.m. - 9 p.m. | FREE |

**1989/90 Nordic Rates**:

| Adult (18-65) | $5 per day |
|---|---|
| Youth (13-17) | $3 per day |
| Seniors (65+) | $3 per day |

# BIG WHITE

Big White Ski Resort
Box 2039, Station R
Kelowna, B.C.,
V1X 4K5

Information: (604)765-3101
Reservations: (604)765-8888
Toll Free (Western Canada-seasonal): 1-800-663-2772

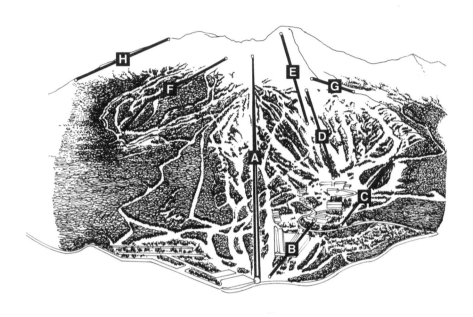

**A** *Ridge Rocket Chair*    **D** *Summit Chair*    **G** *Cliff Platter*
**B** *Plaza Chair*    **E** *Alpine T-bar*    **H** *West Ridge Chair*
**C** *Village Chair*    **F** *Powder Chair*

**How To Get There**: From Highway 97 in Kelowna, follow Highway 33 East 30 km (19 miles) to the Big White turn-off, then 24 km (15 miles) to the Village centre. Good snow tires are required.

**By Air:** Regularly scheduled flights from Vancouver, Calgary and Edmonton via Air B.C., Canadian Airlines International and Time Air. An Airporter service from the Kelowna Airport to Big White can be pre-booked with Big White Central Reservations.

**By Bus:** Greyhound Lines offers scheduled service to Kelowna. Bus passengers can also link up with Airporter Service. Mountainview Bus Lines provides early morning shuttle service to Big White and afternoon return from selected locations throughout Kelowna. Call: (604)765-1800. Special rates for groups.

The title of highest ski resort in British Columbia goes to Big White near Kelowna. Its high elevation means a long ski season and plenty of light, dry snow which, combined with the Okanagan's famous good weather, adds up to great skiing. On top of that, Big White has an excellent on-mountain village that offers everything you could think of to have fun.

Recently Big White opened with $4 million worth of new facilities, including a high-speed quad called the Ridge Rocket, night lighting on the Summit and Village chairlift runs, expansion of the Alpine Centre's entertainment and dining rooms, a new restaurant, additional accommodation and an improved access road. The West Ridge chairlift expands Big White's skiable terrain to over 1,000 acres in an area that provides challenging chutes into Whitefoot Bowl and almost a mile of intermediate fall-line skiing through glades and open trails.

*Powder at Big White.*

The name Big White tells the story; it is big. Its forty-five runs will keep you busy and interested for the entire time you're visiting, and there are never any line-ups. The mountain is almost split in half, with the area above the village mostly beginner and intermediate runs, while over by the Powder chair there is more advanced skiing. But the place to start is the Ridge Rocket quad which opens up a range of ski opportunities. Off to the right you can access the Alpine t-bar which will zip you up to a big, friendly snow bowl or over the ridge to ski the double black diamond Cliff area. On a blue sky day, this is the spot to watch, or join in with, all the hotshots leaping off the ridge against a spectacular backdrop. Where the trees and the bowls meet is snow ghost country. Don't be alarmed, snow ghosts are just snow-encrusted trees that take on new, weird shapes with each passing storm.

Just below the Alpine T-bar is the Summit triple chair that rises from the Alpine Centre area of the village. This lift services a variety of beginner and intermediate runs that will keep you busy for hours. From here, you can still ski over to the Ridge Rocket via the Mogul Track (a green run) or the Villager if you want to explore the rest of the mountain.

The Powder triple chair has some great black diamond runs as well as a couple of intermediates too. Try dropping off Shakey Knees down to Surprise on a powder day for some fun glade skiing. Another area to try for tree skiing is the wide area about half way down the Ridge Rocket on skier's right called Paradise Glades. The name says it all.

Big White's village is spread along the flank of the mountain and surrounded by chair lifts. Just step out the door of your condo, click on your skis and take off. It's as easy as that. People staying in the upper village can either hop on the Summit chair or ski down to the Ridge Rocket. If you want to drop your kids off at ski school or daycare, head for the centre of the village, sign them up and then ski down to the Ridge Rocket via a tunnel under the road and along Hummingbird. You could also board the Village triple chair and then ride up the Summit chair but this route is slower. The Plaza quad chair carries skiers back to the village from the bottom of the Ridge Rocket.

Kids have their own play area and building, Kids Korner, across from the lift ticket office in the centre of the village. The Daycare takes children 18 months and up from 9 a.m to 4:30 p.m. and the certified staff make it fun for the kids with lots of play inside and out. The rates are reasonable and lunch can also be included for a slight extra charge.

Kinderski is for youngsters 3 to 6 who are just starting to ski. It's designed around skiing and snow play for a safe and fun approach. Kid's Klub takes the rest of the kids aged 6 - 12 up the mountain for fun on the runs and provides supervised skiing and instruction. Ski Week packages for Kids Klub and Kinderski can be booked along with lifts and accommodation.

Ski Week packages for adults, youths and juniors include not only instruction but also many special ski week activities. A Welcome Party at the start loosens everyone up. Through the week, join in on movie night, a party for the adults, a Casino night and a talent show for all ages.

There are a number of dining and entertainment choices at Big White. "Get loose with the Moose" for apres ski at the Loose Moose Bar & Grill in the Alpine Centre featuring live entertainment each day from 3:30 p.m. Rose's on the Ridge is a pub, deli and restaurant offering special dinner and banquet parties for groups and families. Snowshoe Sam's bar and restaurant serves all meals. The Whitefoot Dining Lounge & Bistro in the village plaza serves breakfasts and dinners in the licensed dining lounge and lunches and snacks in the licensed Bistro and Coffee Bar.

Perhaps the best evening activity is night skiing on the Village and Summit chairs, Tuesdays through Saturdays from 4:30 to 9:30 p.m.

Big White is reluctant to speak about the ski area's nickname — "Big White Out." Occasionally, but often enough, the clouds descend on the

# BIG WHITE

**Vertical Rise:** 625 m/ 2,050 ft.

**Elevations:** Base 1,661 m/ 5,450 ft.
Top 2,319 m/ 7,606 ft.

| Lifts: | Vertical | Length |
|---|---|---|
| Ridge Rocket Quad | 441 m/ 1,448 ft. | 1,839 m/ 6,033 ft. |
| Plaza Quad Chair | 103 m/ 340 ft. | 700 m/ 2,297 ft. |
| Village Triple Chair | 243 m/ 798 ft. | 996 m/ 3,269 ft. |
| Summit Triple Chair | 259 m/ 850 ft. | 1,048 m/ 3,438 ft. |
| Alpine T-Bar | 301 m/ 990 ft. | 1,283 m/ 4,209 ft. |
| Powder Triple Chair | 303 m/ 995 ft. | 895 m/ 2,939 ft. |
| Cliff Platter | 129 m/ 423 ft. | 293 m/ 961 ft. |

**Lift Capacity:** 12,600 skiers per hour

**Terrain Breakdown:** 35% Beginner
42% Intermediate
23% Advanced

**Total Terrain:** 280 hectares/ 700 acres

**Average Temperature:** -4° C/ 23° F

**Average Snowfall:** 565 cm/ 223 in

**Number of Runs:** 45

**Facilities:** Night skiing, nordic trails, child care, ski shop/rentals, 5 cafeterias/ restaurants, 3 pubs/lounges, ski school, on-mountain accommodation, indoor swimming pool, hot tubs, jacuzzis, saunas, racquetball, grocery store, liquor store, RV hookups, conference and meeting rooms.

**Season Dates:** Mid November to mid April

**Hours of Operation:** Day Skiing 9 a.m. - 3:30 p.m.
Night Skiing 4:30 p.m. - 9:30 p.m. (Tues.-Sat.)

**1990/91 Prices:**

|  | Full Day | Half Day | 9am-9pm | 3:30-9:30 | 12:30-9:30 |
|---|---|---|---|---|---|
| Adult | $32 | $22 | $40 | $16 | $32 |
| Youth | $27 | $19 | $33 | $13 | $27 |
| Child (6-12) | $18 | $13 | $23 | $9 | $18 |
| Senior (65-69) | $22 | $15 | $27 | $11 | $22 |
| Over 70/Under 5 | FREE | | | | |

Lift + accomodation:

| | |
|---|---|
| Adult (18+) | $29 per day |
| Youth (13-17) | $25 per day |
| Child (6-12) | $16 per day |

mountain and turn the visibility to pea soup. That's one of the problems of being high in elevation. If you do stick it out, ski near the trees for reference. Safer bets might be to stay in the restaurants, soak in the outdoor hot tub spa, swim in the indoor pool or play racquetball, none of which sound so bad either.

Twenty-five kilometres (15 miles) of groomed cross country trails and beautiful glades are also waiting out there for your attention and enjoyment. There is no charge, and nordic skiers can access all the trails from the village and have a free uphill return ride on the Plaza quad chairlift. Rentals and repairs are available and maps are at the customer service desk.

One telephone call to the central reservation line will take care of all your booking needs. Some of the perks available are: free night skiing with lift and accommodation packages; free accommodation for children 12 and under with an adult; free skiing for children 5 and under; special junior, youth and senior prices; and special rates for groups with a minimum of 25 people. There are eight hotel/condominium buildings so there will be something to fit your family and your budget. You can ski to and from all accommodation, and in the evenings a free shuttle service from Whitefoot Lodge to the Alpine Centre will take you back up to your room if you come down to the village for dinner. Schedules are posted in the Whitefoot lobby.

Another accommodation option is to stay in Kelowna, 55 minutes away. There are more than 40 hotels or motels offering a wide range of prices and ski packages with daily coach service to Big White. Kelowna has many attractions, including winery tours, museums, night clubs, shopping, art galleries and lots of restaurants. For reservations call (604) 861-5272 from 7 a.m. to 11 p.m. daily, and for the shuttle service call (604)765-1800. Budget car rentals can also provide "skierized" vehicles with pick-up and drop-off in Kelowna or at the airport.

With the new Coquihalla highway connector completed, Kelowna and the Okanagan Valley are only 5 hours from Vancouver. Now more people will find it easier to visit Big White and the other ski resorts in the area. Big White is the premier Okanagan resort with great snow, a modern lift system and the facilities to make your vacation a great one.

# PHOENIX MOUNTAIN

Box 243
Grand Forks, B.C.,
V0H 1H0

(604) 442-2813

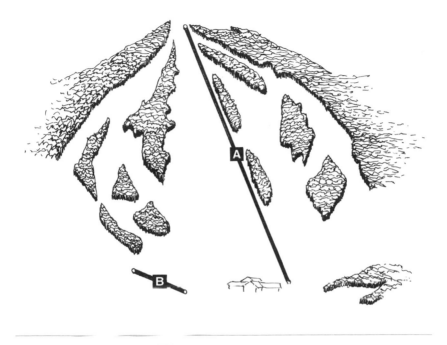

**A** *Face T-bar*        **B** *Rope Tow*

**How To Get There**: Phoenix Ski Hill is 20 minutes west of Grand Forks on Highway 3 and up an 8-km, winding gravel road.

At first glance, Phoenix ski hill can be a little disappointing, but once you recognize it as a community ski hill that serves an enthusiastic local crowd, Phoenix shows its character.

One T-bar, one rope tow, 800 ft. of vertical. That's it. It's not a hill for the destination traveller — but for the kids and families of the area, it's a compact, challenging little mountain. Beside the T-bar line is a steep bump run called the Face. When the T-bar ride is only four minutes to the top, a day of skiing this pitch will have your legs crying for a rest.

Phoenix has an active local race following. They set up gates on Bobcat, an intermediate cruising run, and judging from the number of names on the race list, Phoenix enjoys a solid turnout. For kids keen on ski racing, this hill will force them to learn how to handle their skis.

The rope tow will give the neophytes a chance to practice the basics before heading to the top. There is a small ski school at Phoenix, but make sure you call ahead because the instructors are only around during the busy season. Housed in the same building with the ski school is a retail and rental shop.

Lift tickets and lunch are sold in the gothic arch at the bottom of the T-bar. The cafeteria is fairly limited so you might want to bring your own lunch. And when you need to go to the bathroom, head outside and around the corner of the building. Yes, Phoenix still has outhouses.

The area opened in 1969 when some local people decided they wanted a ski hill. It's a non-profit society and it looks like the minimum has been done to keep it going. That's not a derogatory comment, but when you arrive in the parking lot, it feels like you must have passed through a time warp somewhere along the way.

If you find yourself in Grand Forks in the winter for some reason, try it out. Phoenix Mountain is not a destination ski hill, but it is a great training hill for kids to get the feel of skiing all types of terrain in a low-key atmosphere. A family can still afford to ski here and call it home.

The Providence Lake (also called Marshall Lake) cross country ski area is located off the Phoenix ski hill road. The 17 km of trails were developed by the Kettle Valley Outdoor Club, Katimavik, the Ministry of Forests and other volunteers. There are marked trails as well as old mining roads for the more adventurous. Shelter and toilet facilities are located on the north shore of the lake and are for public use.

## Phoenix Mountain

**Vertical Rise:** 243 m/ 800 ft.

**Elevations:** Base  1,188 m/ 3,900 ft.
Top  1,432 m/ 4,700 ft.

**Lifts:** Face T-bar  (4 minutes to the top)
Rope Tow (Beginner's)

**Terrain Breakdown:** 40% Beginner
40% Intermediate
20% Advanced

**Total Terrain:** 87 acres

**Average Snow:** 120 cm average base

**Number of Runs:** 10

**Facilities:** Coffee Shop, Ski School, Retail Shop

**Season Dates:** Mid-December to mid-March

**Hours of Operation:** 9:00 - 4:00 Saturday/ Sunday
9:30 - 3:30 Weekdays, Christmas to Feb.

**1989/90 Prices:** Weekends  $13.00, Weekdays  $10.00

# SILVER STAR MOUNTAIN

Box 7000
Vernon, B.C.
V1T 8X5

Phone Toll Free: 1-800-663-4431 (Western Canada only)
Snow Phone/Information: (604)542-0224
Vernon: (604)542-1745
Kelowna: (604)860-7827

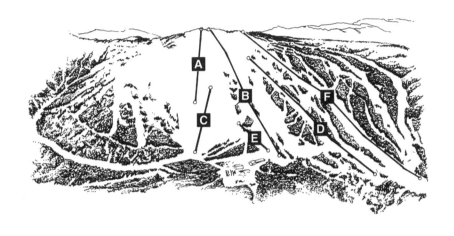

**A** *Hi Tee T-bar*          **C** *Mid-Tee T-bar*          **E** *Town T-bar*
**B** *Summit Chair*          **D** *Aberdeen Chair*          **F** *Vance Creek Chair*

**How To Get There**: Vernon is on Hwy 97 in the Okanagan Valley, centrally located between Vancouver and Calgary. Silver Star is a 22-km drive from Vernon. Canadian Airlines International provides daily service to the Kelowna/Vernon airport from both Calgary and Vancouver. Time Air has regular flights from Lethbridge, Alberta and Vancouver. Air B.C. offers daily departures from Vancouver and Calgary.

A 25-minute limousine service meets all commercial flights and transports passengers to Vernon. Limousine service to the mountain is available on request. Greyhound Lines of Canada provides connections to Vancouver, Prince George, Edmonton and Calgary. By road from Vancouver, follow the Coquihalla Expressway (Hwy 5) leading to Hwy 97 and Vernon. From Calgary, follow the Trans Canada (Hwy 1) to Sicamous and then Hwy 97, south to Vernon.

Silver Star is situated high on a southern plateau 22 km from Vernon. The climate is fairly mild and ideal ski conditions exist between mid-November and late April. They receive consistent snowfalls in the heart of winter which add up, but there are few big snowfalls for powder skiing. It's at its best in the brilliant sunshine of an Okanagan spring.

It's really the village that's the drawing card for Silver Star. It's a piece of the 1890s gas-light era transported to an Okanagan mountainside. The brightly coloured hotels and shops with wooden walkways and wrap-around verandahs form a main street which leads directly to the lifts. This truly is a ski-to-your-door village. A wide range of accommodation is available, each with its own characteristics.

The Vance Creek Hotel is Silver Star's premier hotel. It features a large Victorian-style dining room, a saloon and roof-top hot tubs, and on sunny spring days, its outdoor patio is the place to be. Next door, a swing through the Putnam Hotel and restaurant reveals train whistles, brass punch clocks and old photos covering the walls. The Craigellaiche dining room serves all meals and offers a special children's menu. Visit the Okanagan Valley Cellars downstairs which features local wines and cheeses in a cosy atmosphere.

International mountain guide Klaus Fux and his wife, Annemarie, own the Lord Aberdeen Apartment Hotel, the newest addition to the village. The 13 apartments have comfortable living rooms, kitchens with dishwashers and coffee makers.

A tiny bit of Switzerland lives at the Silver Lode Inn. The traditional European-style rooms and dining room reflect Max and Trudi Schlaepfer's Swiss background. Intricate woodcarving accents the rooms and adds a distinctive flavour.

The Kickwillie Inn and The Pinnacles are located above the village right on the hill. The Kickwillie's seven family suites have private entries, full kitchens and shared use of the roof top hot tubs. The Pinnacles offers 11 deluxe suites with kitchens, sundecks and access to the hot tubs.

There are 47 RV hook-ups adjacent to the village, and washroom and shower facilities are provided in the aquatic centre. Nearby Vernon also has numerous accommodation choices.

As for the skiing, Silver Star is a relatively easy mountain to ski and has mostly beginner and intermediate terrain. There are a few challenging runs like Suicide, Chute and the Face, but the entire area serviced by the Aberdeen and Vance Creek Chairs is all blue and green runs.

On the west ridge though are the "Bus" runs — Outback, Fastback, and Busback. Accessed by the T-bars or Summit Chair, they are inbound, black diamond runs that go beyond the traverse back to the lifts. So on weekends, a bus picks skiers up at the bottom and returns them to the village. Make sure the bus is running before you ski in this area or it's a long walk back.

*Putnam Creek offers challenging terrain.*

Silver Star recognizes its shortcoming in advanced terrain. Traditionally, they have focused on the family ski outing and have done a great job catering to that crowd. But they realize that to keep people coming back, they have to offer more varied terrain. Their answer was the Putnam Creek area. It is mainly intermediate and advanced skiing and extends 305 m (1,000 ft.) below the village elevation for a 762 m (2,500 ft.) vertical drop. It increased Silver Star's skiable terrain by more than 200 per cent.

A high-speed detachable quad services the area and whisks skiers up 2,744 m (9,000 ft.) in 10 minutes. The lift runs down the middle of the area and two ridges, like arms, come around the sides and meet at the bottom of the lift. The south ridge run is for beginners and the north is an intermediate run called Sunny Ridge. Black diamond runs will be cut down the sides of this ridge, with some selective logging to facilitate tree skiing. To top it off, the whole area has great views of the dramatic Monashee Mountains to the east.

For the younger children, there is a playroom open from 8:30 - 12:30 and 1 p.m. - 4 p.m. that is basically a babysitting service. The Stardusters program is for 3 to 8 year olds and covers play and ski instruction. It includes apres-ski activities such as games, movies and visits to the indoor pool at the village's aquatic centre.

Sign up for a ski week and join in on some fun apres-ski as well as five two-hour sessions. There is an adult's program and one for kids under twelve. Silver Star greets you with a wine and cheese reception, and the week ahead includes equipment workshops, movies, bonfires, cross-country skiing night, a fun race and more.

Snowboarders aren't forgotten. A half-pipe and snowboard camps are also available.

## Silver Star Mountain

**Vertical Rise:** 488 m /1,600 ft.

**Elevations:** Village 4,680 ft.
Top  5,620 ft.

| **Lifts:** | Vertical | Length |
|---|---|---|
| Hi-Tee T-Bar | 198 m/ 650 ft. | 670 m/ 2,200 ft. |
| Mid-Tee T-Bar | 152.4 m/ 500 ft. | 609.6 m/ 2,000 ft. |
| Town T-Bar | 61 m/ 200 ft. | 320 m/ 1,050 ft. |
| Summit Chair | 305 m/ 1,000 ft. | 1,220 m/ 4,000 ft. |
| Aberdeen Chair | 335 m/ 1,100 ft. | 1311 m/ 4,300 ft. |
| Vance Creek Chair | 488 m/ 1,600 ft. | 1829 m/ 6,000 ft. |

**Lift Capacity:** 3,500 skiers per hour

**Terrain:** 35% Beginner
50% Intermediate
15% Advanced

**Total Terrain:** 500 hectares

**Average Temperature:** -5° C (20° F)

**Average Base:** 200 cm

**Number of Runs:** 35

**Season Dates:** Mid-November to late April

**Hours of Operation:** Daily 8:30 - 3:30
Night Skiing Tues - Thurs 4:30 - 10 p.m.

**Facilities:** Town Hall Cafeteria (seats 500), playroom, ski shop, ski school, rentals, Ski Patrol, saloon, accommodation, ski & coin lockers.

Aquatic Centre: Heated pool, hot tub, coin laundry, showers & change rooms. Open daily from 2:30 to 9:30 p.m. 1989/90: Adults $2.00; Child $1.00; suit & towel rental $0.50 each. No charge for Silver Star Hotel guests and registered R.V. guests.

RV: Electrical connection sites located in Parking Lot C; Rates (1989/90): $10/ night, $140/ month. All R.V. guests must register at the Skier Services Desk. Shower and washroom facilities are open daily in the Aquatic Centre for R.V. guests 6:00 a.m. to 10:00 a.m.

**Annual Events:** February — Over The Hill Downhill, Beach Party
March — Western Week
Mid April — Funner Daze

## SILVER STAR - CONTINUED

**Area Attractions**: Cedar Hot Springs — Open-year round on Silver Star Road

| 1990/91 Prices: | Full Day | Half Day | Night* |
|---|---|---|---|
| Adult | $32 | $22 | $17 |
| Youth (13-17) | $27 | $22 | $17 |
| Child (6-12) | $18 | $13 | $9 |
| Seniors | $22 | $22 | |
| 5 & Under | FREE | | |
| Cross Country | $6 | | |

*\* Tuesday - Saturday (4:30-10 p.m.)*

The Summit Chair and the T-bar areas are lit for night skiing. If you've never tried it before, don't miss it. Familiar runs suddenly speed up and take on strange aspects. Night skiing makes it feel like a brand new mountain. Something else to consider for evening entertainment is a visit to the Cedar Hot Springs complex on Silver Star Road.

Silver Star also has four kilometres of lit cross country track. During the day, explore the entire nordic system. There are eight kilometres of well-groomed trails at the base of the village and two connector trails lead to another 50 km at the nearby Sovereign Lakes. The trails overlook the Okanagan Valley, and the elevation ensures light, dry snow from mid-November to April. Rentals and lessons are available for both nordic and telemark.

Silver Star is a user-friendly ski area, and the staff tries to make its visiting ski families happy with a welcoming attitude and fun activities. It works.

# Kootenays

*Red Mountain, near Rossland.*

The crème de la crème of powder skiing in B.C. are the two areas in the West Kootenays: Whitewater at Nelson and Red Mountain in Rossland. These are both low-key hills that focus on skiing rather than anything fancy. Steep trees, narrow chutes and bottomless powder are the order of the day. The local ski population is fanatic in its loyalty and love of these areas and likes to keep things quiet, but the word is slowly leaking out to the rest of the world.

Often the months of January and February can seem like one endless powder dump. Snowfalls of twenty to thirty centimetres are common, and with the relatively small skier population of the area, even days after a storm there is still fresh powder waiting in the trees for the first lucky skis to come along. Many articles have been written raving about the incredible conditions, but the Kootenays' curse, or its blessing, is that it's a long way from anywhere. Since it's smack between Calgary and Vancouver, most skiers will turn off to one of the closer resorts rather than drive the extra miles. But if you are a lover of steep powder chutes and perfectly spaced trees, give yourself a treat and make the trip to the Kootenays.

# RED MOUNTAIN

Red Mountain Resorts, Inc.
Box 670
Rossland, B.C.
V0G 1Y0

Central Reservations: 1-800-663-0105
Snowphone: (604)362-5500
Spokane Snowphone: (509)459-6000
(604)362-7384

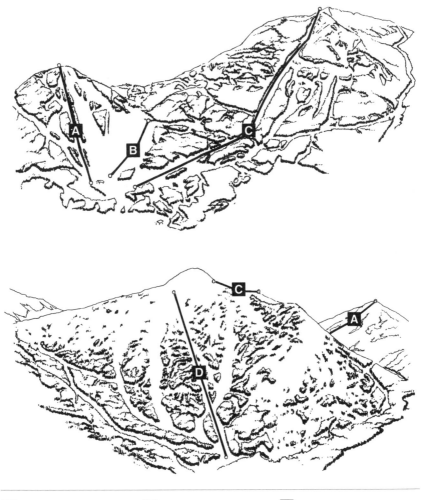

**A** *Red Mountain Chair*   **C** *Granite Mt. Chair*   **D** *Paradise Chair*
**B** *T-bar*

**How To Get There**: Located 3 km (2 miles) west of Rossland in south-eastern B.C., a 10-minute drive north of the U.S. border and 200 km (125 miles) north of Spokane.

Caution: Skiing spoken here. Rossland is one of the few remaining ski bum havens. It has always been famous for copious amounts of light, champagne powder snow, steep chutes and great tree skiing. It still is.

The first time I skied powder over my head was at Red Mountain. A long-time patroller at the area took us to some chutes that changed my whole perception of skiing. Trees spaced just far enough apart opened into unexpected glades then closed in again to another cat and mouse line. Lumps and bumps exploded and choked me with snow. A sudden drop and I was submerged, blinded, bursting out the far side, whooping with excitement, the burning in my thighs overridden by rampant adrenaline. A last rush through and out onto Long Squaw for a cruise to the bottom of Granite Chair.

The ski area, though called Red Mountain, is actually home to two mountains — Red and Granite. Since Rossland's early mining days, enthusiastic skiers have taken advantage of the area's abundant snowfalls. In 1897, Red Mountain hosted the first Canadian Ski Jumping and Ski Racing Championships, both won by local Olaus Jeldness, a Scandinavian miner and the instigator of skiing in Rossland.

The first chairlift in Western Canada was put up at Red in 1947 by the local ski society, and in 1965 a double chair was installed on neighbouring Granite Mountain. Red is the mountain where 26 members of the National Ski Team, such as Nancy Greene, Felix Belczyk, Diana Haight and Don Stevens, honed their technique. Even the calibre of the local skiers is first class. Once you ski these mountains, you'll understand why they turn out so many skilled skiers.

The ski area is only a five-minute drive from Rossland. Red Mountain rears its head above the parking lot with a double chair rising 435 m (1,420 ft.) to its steep dome. If the bumps on Upper War Eagle and the Cliff make your knees ache just looking at them, there's always the Back Trail to descend. The trees dropping off below Salley's Alley to Dale's Trail are a more challenging route to the bottom.

Neighbouring Granite Mountain towers over Red. It's a long, 18-minute chair ride to the top, but it covers 2,500 m (8,200 ft.). There is a long, flat area at the bottom of the mountain before the steep top two-thirds. Sun-drenched Paradise triple chair on the back of Granite accesses 415 m (1,350 ft.) of great intermediate cruising and bumps. To perfect your groomed skiing techniques, head for Southern Belle and Southern Comfort. Ruby Tuesday and Meadows aren't usually groomed so are bumpy black diamond runs and if you duck between these cut runs, you'll find lots of fun trees to play in. Long Squaw is a gentle road from the top of Granite Chair, past the top of Paradise area and winding down to the bottom of the mountain. South Side Road is the easy way out of Paradise.

Expert tree skiers are in heaven on Granite. When you get off the Granite Chair, head to the right and down Buffalo Ridge. Ski straight along (don't turn down the steep pitch on Main) and follow the trail until it opens out below you. This area is called the Slides and is steep,

gladed tree skiing with lots of open areas. Catch this on a powder day — fantastic! You'll hook up with Long Squaw at the bottom which takes you back to Granite Chair. The great thing about Granite is that you'll always end up on Long Squaw or South Side Road back to the bottom.

For ski tourers who are knowledgeable and familiar with out-of-bounds skiing, the mountains beside Red and Granite offer some of the most accessible touring around. A 25-minute tour up Roberts, off the back of Granite, brings you out on a ridge that drops off to exciting chutes and trees. At the bottom, ski right to the Paradise Chair. Make sure you check with the ski patrol about avalanche conditions and be

*Try some of the steep chutes at Red.*

prepared. Pick up a $5 single-ride ticket if you will only be touring and not using the lifts for more than the ride up Granite.

Don't get the impression that Red Mountain and the area caters only to expert skiers. There is lots of room for beginners and children. On the shoulder of Red Mountain is a 610 m (2,900 ft.) T-bar that rises 137 m (450 ft.). A very wide run here gives everyone space to practice and play.

The ski school has a number of packages that offer something for every level. A Never-Ever special package will get the first-time skier up and started inexpensively. The "REDiscover Red Week" (Club Red) runs for four days and includes four lessons, on-mountain brunch, video analysis, fun race and group photo. It's a great way to improve your skiing and make new friends. Red also has 50+ Skiing packages, a Ladies Day program and Powder Passion to teach you how to deal with all the deep snow.

## RED MOUNTAIN

**Vertical Rise:** 853 m/ 2,800 ft.

**Elevations:** Base 1,160 m/ 3,800 ft.
Top 2,102 m/ 6,600 ft. (4th largest vertical drop in B.C.)

| Lifts: | Vertical | Length |
|---|---|---|
| Red Mountain Chair | 435 m/ 1,420 ft. | 1,200 m/ 3,900 ft. |
| T-Bar | 137 m/ 4,50 ft. | 610 m/ 2,900 ft. |
| Granite Mtn. Chair | 850 m/ 2,800 ft. | 2,500 m/ 8,200 ft. |
| Paradise Chair | 415 m/ 1,350 ft. | 1,100 m/ 3,600 ft. |

**Lift Capacity:** 3,000 skiers per hour

**Terrain Breakdown:** 30% Beginner
35% Intermediate
35% Expert
Expert off-run skiing

**Total Terrain:** 2,000 acres

**Average Temp:** 25° F

**Average Snowfall:** 750 cm/ 300 in.

**Number of Runs:** 30

**Season Dates:** Mid-November to mid-April

**Hours of Operation:**
Granite Chair 9 a.m. - 3:30 p.m.
Red Chair 10 a.m. - 2 p.m.
No night skiing

**Facilities:** Base Lodge - Rafters Pub, Luigi's Pizza & Mexican Food, Cafeteria

**Special Events:**
Club Red: Four days of ski lessons, guiding and video analysis with an on-mountain brunch, welcome reception, group photo session and more.

| 1990/91 Prices | Full Day | Half Day |
|---|---|---|
| Adult | $30 | $24 |
| Youth/Student (13-18) | $25 | $20 |
| Child (7-12) | $14 | $11 |
| Seniors | $18 | $13 |
| 6 & Under | FREE | |
| One Ride Ticket | $5 | |

For a change of pace, the Black Jack Cross Country Ski Club, located near the base of Red Mountain, offers 40 km of mechanically set trails, with two diagonal tracks, one skating lane and three huts. The trails form a network of loops for all abilities and pass through varied terrain, from open beaver ponds and homestead sites to thick stands of hemlocks. The group is a non-profit organization and depends on skier support to keep operating. Phone (604)362-5811 for more information.

Red Mountain Kinder Care is located in the gothic arch building on the access road from the highway. It is only a three minute walk from the base lodge. It is open from 8:30 a.m. to 3:30 p.m. and takes care of children aged 18 months to 6 years. Call (604)362-7112 for more information.

The Sunshine Cafe on Columbia Avenue has been the locals' favourite since it opened and with just cause. It serves great food at reasonable prices. Two new restaurants opened recently — Rockingham's on Columbia, with an extensive menu and a happening atmosphere, and The Flying Steamshovel on Washington Street. Both are more upscale than the Sunshine and serve good food as well. The Louis Blue restaurant in the Uplander Hotel is the most expensive, and the atmosphere is a little stiff compared to the rest of Rossland, but the chef likes to experiment so you may find that Thai food is the special of the evening.

The Flying Steamshovel also houses the Only Well Pub, a good spot after a day on the hill, while the Powder Keg Pub in the Uplander has live bands and a dance floor. The After The Goldrush Cafe is a combination book store/cappuccino bar on Washington Street. Every third Sunday they host a coffee house, and some of the local talent bring their guitars, poems and humour along for an entertaining evening.

Traditionally skiers have stayed at the Red Shutter Inn or the Ram's Head Inn, both located at the base of the hill and offering good home-cooked meals. Recently a number of enterprising locals have converted their homes into bed and breakfasts. There is Carolyn's at the base of Red Mountain and Angela's Place and the Tinker's Hatch in town. Call the central reservation line at 1-800-663-0105 for more information.

The new owners of the hill have plans to expand the ski facilities which would only improve on an already good thing. The area may be difficult to get to, but the bottom line is simple — it's worth it. Only time will tell how much development will actually take place, but after skiing Red Mountain and enjoying the warm atmosphere of Rossland, it was hard not to stay and ski here forever.

# WHITEWATER

Whitewater Ski Resort Ltd.
Box 60
Nelson, B.C.
V1L 5P7

Information/Reservations (604)354-4944
Snowphone: (604)352-7669
Calgary Snowphone: (403)269-1133

**A** *Hummingbird Chair*     **B** *Silver King T-bar*     **C** *Summit Chair*

**How To Get There**: Whitewater is located in the Selkirk Range in southeastern B.C., 19 km (12 miles) south of Nelson on Hwy 6.
Access: By Time Air and Air B.C. to Castlegar, or by bus or car to Nelson. Distance from Vancouver, 620 km (400 miles).

Free-fall tree skiing and abundant white velvet snow make Whitewater famous in the powder underground. Combine these ingredients with the beautiful heritage town of Nelson and you'll find the perfect destination for the advanced skier searching for an out-of-the-way holiday.

For skiers the situation at Whitewater is perfect: tons of snow, challenging terrain and no crowds. Who would really expect many people to make the long trek to this small ski area in the Kootenays? Perhaps Ski Canada magazine's description of Whitewater as "the best day-to-day, lift-serviced powder (in Canada)" will be inspiration for a road trip.

Spectacular Ymir Peak, anchoring the high basin the ski area is nestled in, is largely responsible for the abundant snow Whitewater receives. At 2,400 m (8,000 ft.), Ymir (pronounced Wymer) rakes the clouds of any flakes of snow they may be holding and mixes up white water or $WH_2O$ (the powder formula). Also, Whitewater's base is at 1,640 m (5,400 ft.) which puts it well into the light and dry zone. The season lasts from November to early April, and the top base annually receives more than 700 cm (22 ft.). The area closes relatively early because of a lack of skiers, not a lack of snow.

*Try the great tree skiing at Whitewater.*

Whitewater has been around for about 17 years but has only been discovered in the last few years. A rise in Nelson's profile, 20 km away, has been a boost. The "Queen City of the Kootenays" has great pride in its heritage and has restored many of the grand Victorian buildings. In 1986, Nelson was the setting for two popular movies. *Roxanne*, starring Steve Martin and Darryl Hannah, and *Housekeeping*, an award-winning Canadian picture, were both filmed here.

On paper Whitewater seems small. It has the beginner's Hummingbird chair and the Silver King T-bar, but it's the large area of skiable terrain accessible from the Summit Chair that gives the hill its reputation. Endless lines through the trees along the ridge plus the few cut runs could keep you busy all season within the ski hill boundaries.

The north-facing Summit Chair offers a 400m (1,300 ft.) vertical drop for intermediate and advanced skiers. The Summit Chair lift line, called the Blast, is a mogul-basher paradise. Steep, long and gnarly, this run will draw every ounce of energy you can muster. To the right, Diamond Drill, Dynamite and Glory Basin are all bump runs that join up to a traverse at the bottom which zips you back to the lift. In between these runs are the famous trees of Whitewater. These are probably some of the trickier trees going because there are drop offs and narrow lines which demand precision and confidence. Tree skiing is not for beginners or those unfamiliar with the mountain.

## WHITEWATER

**Vertical Rise**: 400 m/ 1,300 ft.

**Elevations**: Base 1,640 m/ 5,400 ft.
Top 2,040 m/ 6,700 ft.

| **Lifts**: | Vertical | Length |
|---|---|---|
| Hummingbird Chair | 76 m/ 250 ft. | 457 m/ 1,500 ft. |
| Silver King T-bar | 182 m/ 600 ft. | 548 m/ 1,800 ft. |
| Summit Double Chair | 396 m/ 1,300 ft. | 944 m/ 3,100 ft. |

**Lift Capacity**: 3,000 skiers per hour

**Terrain Breakdown**: 50% Expert
30% Int.
20% Beginner

**Total Terrain**: 2,000 acres

**Avg. Temperature**: -4° C January/ February

**Avg. Snowfall**: 700 cm/ 22 ft.

**Number of Runs**: 21 runs; Open and treed slopes, beginner's slope near lodge

**Season Dates**: November to early April

**Hours of Operation**: 9:00 - 3:30

**Facilities**: Shucky's Cafeteria, Coal Oil Johnny's Saloon, Ski school, ski shop, ski rentals.

| **1990/91 Prices\***: | Full Day | Half Day |
|---|---|---|
| Adult | $23.50 | $18.20 |
| Youth (13-18) | $20.30 | $15.00 |
| Child(7-12) | $15.00 | $11.75 |
| Seniors | $20.30 | $15.00 |
| 6 & Under | FREE | |
| 3 Day adult ticket | $65.00 | |

*For groups of 25 or more - $19/ person/ day*

On the other side of the basin is a series of runs serviced by the Silver King T-bar. There are two beginner runs, Sluice Box and Yankee Girl which funnel down to the wide-open Hummingbird run and back to the lodge. Motherlode and Bonanza are the cruising runs on the mountain. They are wide with the odd steeper pitch thrown in to keep you on your toes. I often saw little kids and learners on these runs so don't be intimidated. To the left of the T-bar are six ungroomed runs that are rated black diamond. Compared to the other black diamond runs on the hill, these are easier. They are all open runs, fairly steep and probably the best place on the mountain to find your powder legs and practice skiing in the trees. The ski school offers good programs so you can soon get out there and rip it up with the rest.

The atmosphere at Whitewater is relaxed and low-key. Every afternoon in Coal Oil Johnny's Saloon, skiers gather for a warming coffee drink and to listen to some local talent onstage. The food served at Shucky's, also in the main lodge, is as good as the skiing.

There are extensive cross country trails located across from the Whitewater turn-off on Highway 6. The Nelson Nordic Touring Centre maintains several groomed trails in the Apex Valley. The Camp Busk area is a 7-km loop from the Whitewater Inn, a bed and breakfast across the highway, to the old Euphrates mine. Two hill sections make it an intermediate trail. The Apex trail is a gentle three-km loop around a large open meadow. No hills on this one. The Cottonwood Lake trail extends north from the Apex loop three km and is rated moderate.

Nelson is only 20 minutes from the ski hill, and it's worth spending some time exploring this heritage town. More than fifty buildings were restored in the early 1980s, and the citizens carried on the trend by restoring many of the homes to their original beauty. Nelson feels different from anywhere else in B.C. It has some kind of magic that will touch you as soon as you arrive.

The Heritage Inn offers bed and breakfast at $20 for two people. The opaque glass standing lamps, old-style furnishings and the huge clawfoot bath tubs down the hall will bring out the romantic in you. This building also houses Mike's Place, a popular pub with big TV screens and a pool table, and the Boiler Room, visited by the younger crowd. As a result, some rooms in the inn may be noisy. There are lots of standard motels in Nelson. The Alpine Motel is on the route out of town to the ski hill. That'll save you five minutes on a big powder day. The Villa Motel and the North Shore Inn are both across the bridge on Hwy 3A and provide nice views of the West Arm of Kootenay Lake and the city.

A couple of places to recommend for food are the Main Street Diner on Baker Street and Le Chatelet at the foot of the orange bridge. The first serves up good burgers and the like in a casual atmosphere, and the second is a welcoming French restaurant featuring brick-oven-baked specialities and delicate salads.

An enjoyable side trip is a visit to Ainsworth Hot Springs, about 45 minutes from Nelson on Highway 3A. The hot springs are open year round with a hotel, restaurant and swimming pool.

Many a week-long ski holiday has turned into a lifetime love affair with the Kootenays. The great snow, low-key atmosphere and warmth of the people make this hidden corner of B.C. a favourite place to visit.

# Rockies

*The powder bowls at Fernie Snow Valley attract skiers from around the world.*

The Rocky Mountain Trench is home to five ski resorts, making it the perfect area for an easy hill-to-hill road trip. Fernie Snow Valley, Fairmont Hot Springs, Kimberley, Panorama and Whitetooth all provide exciting challenges for noviuce, intermediate and advanced skiers.

Each area is only an hour or so from the next, providing you with the opportunity to sample some diverse ski experiences without having to travel great distances to the next stop.

Although the location of these resorts, within a few hours of Calgary, makes them favourites of Alberta skiers, they are well worth the trip for Vancouver skiers looking for new skiing territory.

# FAIRMONT HOT SPRINGS

Box 10
Fairmont Hot Springs, B.C.
V0B 1L0

Toll Free Reservations: 1-800-663-4979
Calgary Direct Phone: (403)264-0746 or (403)264-6061
Information: (604)345-6311

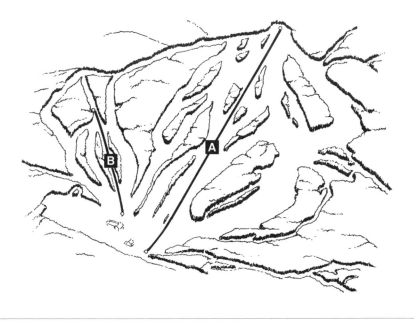

**A** *Sundance Chair*     **B** *Snowbird Platter*

**How To Get There**: Fairmont Hot Springs is located on Highway 95 in the Rocky Mountain Trench in southeastern B.C. The resort is 305 km (190 miles) from Calgary and 915 km (570 miles) from Vancouver.

*By Air:* Cranbrook - 80 km (50 miles) - Daily service via Canadian Airlines International; Calgary - Daily service via Air Canada, Canadian Airlines International, American, Delta and other carriers; Fairmont - Service by air charter or private aircraft to the resort.

*By Bus:* Daily Greyhound service from Calgary and Cranbrook.

The Kootenai Indians first discovered the soothing mineral springs at the western base of the Rocky Mountains generations ago. Since 1922, under the Wilder family's direction, thousands of people have migrated each year to Fairmont to enjoy the hot springs complemented by golf or skiing. Fairmont Hot Springs is a great family resort for skiers and non-skiers alike. The ski hill is especially suited to beginners and intermediates, so relax, ski a bit and soak a lot.

## FAIRMONT HOT SPRINGS

**Vertical Rise:** 304 m/ 1,000 ft.
**Elevations:** Base 1,280 m/ 4,200 ft.
Top 1,584 m/ 5,200 ft.
**Lifts:** Sundance Triple Chair
Snowbird Platter Lift
**Lift Capacity:** 2,400 skiers per hour
**Terrain Breakdown:** 20% Beginner
65% Intermediate
15% Advanced
**Number of Runs:** 10
**Facilities:** Day lodge, Canada's largest natural hot springs, recreation facilities, grocery store, liquor store, post office, RV hookups, conference facilities, laundromat, massage therapist, lounge, restaurant, Child care, ski shop, rentals, ski school, snowmaking, children's play area, cross-country ski trails.
**Season Dates:** Mid-December to Easter
**Hours of Operation:** 9:30 a.m. - 4 p.m.
February - Night skiing Friday evenings until 9 p.m.

| 1990/91 Prices*: | Full Day | Half Day | 3 Day | Sunday |
|---|---|---|---|---|
| Adult | $22 | $16 | $55 | $16 |
| Youth (9-14) | $15 | $11 | $36 | $11 |
| Child (8 & Under) | FREE | | | |
| Seniors (65+) | FREE | | | |

*All lift tickets include one free swim in the public hot pools*

The springs really are the major draw to Fairmont. Every day more than 4.5 million litres (990,000 gallons) of hot water bubble up to fill Canada's largest natural hot pool complex. There are three pools of clear, odourless hot mineral water with temperatures ranging from 35 - 45° C (90 - 106° F) that offer ideal shallow areas for children and soakers and 25-metre lanes for swimmers. Fairmont Lodge guests have exclusive use of a fourth, smaller outdoor hot pool, indoor hot soak pool, cold plunge pool and saunas.

The ski area, located threee kilometres (1.5 miles) from Fairmont Lodge is primarily an intermediate family area that promotes fun, ski racing, ski improvement courses and packages. The triple chair and platter lift are more than adequate to service the area's 300 m (1,000 ft.) of vertical. In late winter, the triple chair is open for night skiing on Friday evenings. Snowmaking on 60 per cent of the mountain ensures good consistent snow conditions from December to April. The large day chalet, with a sundeck and spectacular view of the Rockies, houses a cafeteria, lounge, ticket office, ski school, babysitting and ski patrol.

The Fairmont Ski School offers a high level of ski coaching and instruction with 10 full and part time CSIA (Canadian Ski Instructors Alliance) ski pros to teach all levels. The most popular ski packages are those with lessons and the Christmas racing camp for children. Specialized how-to-ski Snowbird programme for 4 to 8 year olds and the Nancy Greene fun racing for 6 to 14 year olds will keep all the kids learning and happy.

The country-style Fairmont Lodge has 140 rooms with view balconies and complimentary use of all pools. In addition, there are 96 one- and two-bedroom villas bordering Fairmont's Mountainside Golf course. The R.V. park is conveniently located next to the Lodge and pools, with over 30 year-round full-service sites. Many accommodation packages are available, so phone the resort for the details.

Fairmont Hot Springs Resort also offers the services of two full-time massage therapists trained in hydrotherapy and massage. Make an appointment for a therapy session or book a full spa program for groups of six to fifteen participants.

A sports centre rounds out the non-skiing activity choices and features two racquetball courts, a squash court, a large mirrored fitness room with hydrafitness equipment, a fun pool, indoor and outdoor jacuzzis and relaxation rooms with a fireplace. Daily aerobic and aquacise classes are offered, and all facilities are available for a nominal daily fee or are included with certain ski packages.

With this range of services, it is easy to see why Fairmont Hot Springs Resort is an ideal vacation spot for the whole family, skiers and non-skiers alike.

# FERNIE SNOW VALLEY

Box 788
Fernie, B.C.
V0B 1M0

General Information: (604)423-4655
On Mountain Reservations: (604)423-9221
Central Reservations (Fernie): (604)423-9284

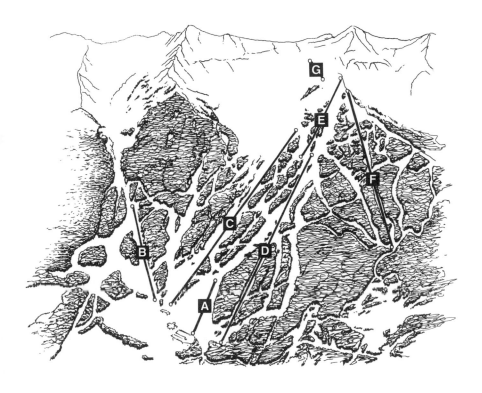

| **A** *Bunny Tow* | **D** *El Quad Chair* | **F** *Boomerang Chair* |
|---|---|---|
| **B** *Deer T-bar* | **E** *Bear T-bar* | **G** *Face Lift* |
| **C** *Griz Chair* | | |

**How To Get There**: Fernie is located in the southeast corner of the B.C Rockies on Crowsnest Hwy #3. It is 60 km west of the Alberta border and 60 km north of the U.S. border. Snow Valley ski resort is 5 km from the town of Fernie.

Serviced by Greyhound Bus Lines twice daily and daily flights into Cranbrook (1 hour away) by Time Air and Air B.C.

*Great terrain and lots of snow can be found at Fernie Snow Valley.*

There's a perfectly logical explanation for all the snow that Fernie receives. It's because of the mythical man, Griz. As the legend goes, a baby boy was born in a bear's den back in the cruel winter of 1879. When the bear woke in the spring, it quickly became a coat to keep the boy warm. Rumours passed for years among the local mountaineers of a man who lived in the hills, had shoulders six feet wide, an eight foot musket and wore a bear skin coat and cap. Most people just thought the stories were fictional - that is, until recently.

Some ski tourers were in the peaks above Snow Valley in a heavy snow storm. During a break in the weather, they noticed a man in a bear skin coat standing on the peak shooting his musket into the clouds. Every time he fired, more snow fell. He was quickly lost amid the thick snow but the skiers could still hear the muffled echo of his musket through the storm.

Whether it's because of Griz or not, Fernie does get a mountain of snow. And what's even better, they have the terrain to really ski it up.

Fernie Snow Valley was ideally designed by Nature to become a ski hill. The Lizard Range is spectacular. The peaks form a jagged crown and drop away to expansive powder bowls. The steep upper slopes gradually soften, and the lower mountain provides gentler terrain for novice and intermediate skiers.

The snow falls from late December to early March, and bring your snorkel because it's light and dry. The best places to find all that powder are in Lizard and Cedar Bowls. Ride the El Quad Chair half way up the mountain and then ski down to the Boomerang Chair and then up to Cedar Bowl and the North Ridge area or go left to the Bear T-Bar and the Face Lift handle tow to access Lizard Bowl.

## FERNIE SNOW VALLEY

**Vertical Rise:** 730 m/ 2,400 ft.

**Elevations:** Base 1,067 m/ 3,500 ft.
Top 1,798 m/ 5,900 ft.

| Lifts: | Length | Vertical |
|---|---|---|
| Bunny Tow | 150 m/ 500 ft. | |
| Deer T-Bar | 650 m/ 2,130 ft. | 140 m/ 460 ft. |
| Griz Double Chair | 1,540 m/ 5,050 ft. | 320 m/ 1,060 ft. |
| El Quad Chair | 1,410 m/ 4,630 ft. | 310 m/ 1,020 ft. |
| Bear T-Bar | 900 m/ 2,970 ft. | 310 m/ 1,020 ft. |
| Boomerang Triple Chair | 1,230 m/ 4,040 ft. | 500 m/ 1,640 ft. |
| Face Lift | 300 m/ 1,000 ft. | 100 m/ 330 ft. |

**Lift Capacity:** 7,000 skiers per hour

**Terrain Breakdown:** 25% Beginner
40% Intermediate
35% Advanced

**Average Temperature:** -2° C

**Average Snowfall:** 450 cm/ 15 ft. Average 300 - 350 cm base

**Number of Runs:** 40 defined runs, 2 alpine bowls

**Season Dates:** Mid-November to end of April

**Hours of Operation:** 9:30 - 4:00 weekdays
9:00 - 4:00 weekends/holidays
10:00 - 3:00 Christmas Day

**Facilities:** Cafeteria, Pizza Pit Restaurant, Griz Inn for sit down service, Bear's Inn snack bar at top of quad chair, On-hill accommodation, child care facilities, ski shop, ski rentals, ski school, 2 pubs, 1 lounge, grocery store, RV hookups, conference and meeting rooms.

**Special Events:** February - Powder 8 Championships, Griz Days Festival
April - Annual Scavenger Hunt, Powder-Pedal-Paddle Relay Race
May - Spring Ski Fiesta

| 1990/91 Prices*: | Full Day | Half Day | 3 Day | 5 Day |
|---|---|---|---|---|
| Adult | $27 | $21 | $72 | $110 |
| Youth (13-17) | $20 | $15 | $57 | $85 |
| Child (7-12) | $10 | $10 | $30 | $50 |
| Seniors | $20 | $15 | | |
| 6 & Under | FREE | | | |
| Cross Country Trails | FREE | | | |

*Multi Day Passes any consecutive days except Dec. 22 - Jan. 7*

*Group Discounts for 20 or more. Organizer skis FREE*

*Fernie Fanatic Pass: Purchase frequent skier discount pass for $25 and ski for only $19 per day.*

Neither area is all that difficult. They're open bowls with some steeper knolls but there's always an easier option. Lizard Bowl even has some green runs while Cedar has intermediate and advanced skiing. The treed area beside the Bear T-bar is definitely challenging, and Snake Ridge on the far side of Cedar Bowl is rated a double black diamond. All skiers, except for absolute beginners, should be able to try out the powder skiing on a run they find comfortable.

Novice skiers will feel more comfortable skiing the El Quad, the Griz Chair and the Deer T-bar areas which have much more suitable terrain. The Deer T-bar is particularly good because there is only one run that feeds into it from above so it's almost like a separate area.

The ski school offers programs to advance all levels of skiers. The Ski Wizards drop-in program is designed for three to six years and seven to thirteen years. For the younger group, the lessons include on-slope ski games and teaching exercises where the priorities are fun, safety and ski improvement. The children are divided into three categories of ability so everyone skis at their own level. Just drop by the Ski School half an hour before lesson time and buy a ticket. Snow Valley also has a 1,500-square-foot nursery with a nap room for the really young kids.

Back-country touring is popular at Fernie. Currie Bowl and Timber Bowl are over the ridge to the west of the ski hill and are easily accessible. Lifts are proposed for each that would double the area of Snow Valley but nothing is firm about these plans at present. Be aware that these areas are out of bounds and are not patrolled by the ski area. Be prepared.

Fernie also has cross country ski trails which extend from both sides of the base area. They wind along the lower slopes of the mountain so expect a good cardio-vascular work-out. While there are no lit tracks for night skiing, a great evening (and daytime) activity is to go for a horse-drawn sleigh ride. It's only $5 a person and kids under three ride free. Call (604)529-7795 or the Griz Inn.

Snow Valley's weakness, for a family vacation, is the shortage of on-hill accommodation. The Griz Inn, a new 35-room hotel, and RV hook-ups in the upper parking lot are all there is. The Griz has attractive one- to three-bedroom condominiums with full kitchens and has a restaurant, lounge, sauna, jacuzzi and banquet room. The RV hook-ups are $10 per night (1989-90), and there are shower and washroom facilities. Fernie is only five minutes away and has a number of motels and hotels. Call central reservations at (604)423-9221.

Fernie Snow Valley is an unknown treasure. It's not flashy and isn't one of the "in" places to ski, but for powder snow, mild temperatures and friendly people, it's near the top of the list. If you're lucky, you might be there when Griz is stomping around in the peaks, unleashing more of the famous Fernie powder.

# KIMBERLEY

Kimberley Ski and Summer Resort
Box 40, Kimberley, B.C.
V1A 2Y5

Information & Snow Phone: (604)427-4881
Calgary: (403)269-1133
Reservations: (604)427-5385
Toll-free Reservations, December - March: 1-800-663-4755

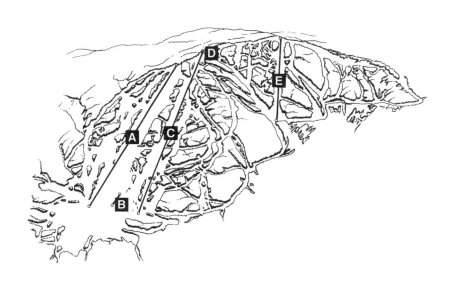

**A** *Maverick T-bar*     **C** *Buckhorn Chair*     **E** *Easter Chair*
**B** *Pony Tow*           **D** *Pony Tow*

**How To Get There**: Kimberley is located in the southeast corner of B.C. on Highway 95A. There is Greyhound service daily from Calgary and Vancouver. Cranbrook Airport is only 20 km away with daily service via Time Air and Air B.C. Rental cars are available or a ski-area shuttle can be arranged through accommodation reservations. International connections are available via Calgary and Vancouver.

The Kimberley Ski and Summer Resort on North Star Mountain has everything a family looks for in a vacation: good weather, varied ski terrain, on-hill accommodation, organized activities and child care. The resort is located inside the city limits of Kimberley, also known as the "Bavarian City of the Rockies," for its European architecture. The ski hill is only a five-minute drive from the Platzl, Kimberley's downtown outdoor pedestrian mall.

Kimberley's history is tightly woven with the activity at the Sullivan Mine, once the world's richest silver, lead and zinc mine. The town was even named after Kimberley, South Africa, also a famous mining area. The Sullivan Mine has had a roller coaster life, and when its resources began to dwindle again in the 1970s, the town adopted the Bavarian theme to boost its economy through tourism. As a result, the Kimberley Ski and Summer Resort has become one of the main anchors of the local economy.

North Star Mountain has been in operation for over 25 years. It's a well-laid-out mountain and offers a wide array of skiing terrain, from easy cruising on wide groomed runs serviced by the Maverick T-bar and the Buckhorn double chair to the bumps and steeper runs of the Easter triple chair. A new lift, the Rosa triple chair, has gone up beside the t-bar and greatly increases the access to these beginner and intermediate runs. The Easter Chair accesses the higher slopes and black diamond runs on the northern side of the resort. There is only one beginner run, Ridgeway, in this area and a couple of intermediate pitches off to the

*North Star Mountain.*

right of the Easter Chair. If you're looking for some wild bumps, try out Magma or Vortex. Even the names let you know you'd better look before you leap.

Kimberley also has some good glade skiing, especially when the area has received new snow. A pitch called All Over Glade, along the ridge to the left of the Easter chair, is a short, fun run down to Caper and back to the chair. A little bit tougher (black diamonds) are Dinkum and Quantrell, both off Stemwinder, which offer steep pitches through spaced trees. Kimberley seldom receives huge dumps of powder; instead they get steady, smaller amounts that provide a good base.

A great way to familiarize yourself with the mountain is to meet up with the guest guides. Local skiers who know the mountain take visitors on personalized tours every day at 10 a.m., 12 noon and 1 p.m. Meet at the large resort map next to the ticket office for this free service.

Kimberley offers a full array of ski school programs tailored to fit any ability. Group lessons are held daily at 11 a.m. and 1:30 p.m. and private lessons are available by appointment. Ski Scamps are a snow-play session on skis for kids aged 5 and under, and the "7 Eleven" Ski Heaven is

## KIMBERLEY

**Vertical Rise**: 702 m/ 2,300 ft.

**Elevations**: Base 1,280 m/ 4,200 ft.
Top  1,982 m/ 6,500 ft.

| Lifts: | Vertical | Length |
|---|---|---|
| Maverick T-bar | 487 m/ 1,600 ft. | 1,828 m/ 6,000 ft. |
| Pony Tow | 62 m/ 200 ft. | 212 m/ 700 ft. |
| Buckhorn Double Chair | 548 m/ 1,800 ft. | 2,134 m/ 7,000 ft. |
| Pony Tow | 31 m/ 100 ft. | 150 m/ 500 ft. |
| Easter Triple Chair | 365 m/ 1,000 ft. | 1,098 m/ 3,600 ft. |

**Lift Capacity**: 4,200 skiers per hour

**Terrain Breakdown**: 20% Beginner
60% Intermediate
20% Advanced

**Total Amt of Terrain**: 425 acres of skiable terrain within 1,200 acres of resort area

**Average Temperature**: -5° C/ 23° F

**Average Snowfall**: 300 cm/ 120 in.

**Average Base**: 110 cm/ 45 in.

**Number of Runs**: 34

**Facilities**: Night skiing, ski rentals, ski shop, ski school, cafeteria, restaurants, accommodation, conference facilities, racquet centre, childcare, saunas, hot tubs, ice skating.

**Season Dates**: December to mid-April

**Hours of Operation**: Night Skiing
Tuesday through Saturday, 5 - 10 p.m.

**Snowmaking**: 75% of Main run, 15% of resort

**Special Events**: February—Winterfest, 5 days with beerfests, casinos and a talent showcase. Play winter sports in the day and dance at night.

| 1990/91 Prices*: | Full Day | Half Day | 3 Day | 5 Day |
|---|---|---|---|---|
| Adult | $29.95 | $22.50 | $83.50 | $133.75 |
| Youth (13-18) | $26.00 | $19.00 | $71.00 | $112.50 |
| Child (9-12) | $15.00 | $11.75 | $51.50 | $80.25 |
| Seniors | $19.00 | $12.50 | | |
| 8 & Under | FREE | | | |

*Night Skiing: Tuesday through Saturday - included in day ticket*

for kids only, ages 12 and under. One of the most popular ski programs is the two- and four-day, all-inclusive Klub Kimberley and Kids Klub Kimberley, featuring ski workshops, video sessions, action photos and steak barbecue buffet. Kimbercare offers fully qualified supervision of 2 to 6 year olds with a program to suit different age groups, outdoor play and optional ski lessons. This service operates daily from 9 a.m. to 4:30 p.m. throughout the ski season, and daycare is available through Guest Services in the summer months. For more information about Kimbercare, call (403)427-4881, extension 611.

For the cross country skiers in your group, the entrance to 26 km of groomed and track-set trails is directly opposite the Kirkwood Inn. These trails are suitable for all levels and a 3.5 km loop is lit until 10 p.m. for night skiing.

The resort has a good range of dining spots to choose from. There are five buildings between the T-bar and the Buckhorn chair that make up the base area. Here you'll find the North Star Day Lodge which contains a cafeteria and the Miner's Den Dining Room. The North Star Centre next door is the site for the North Star Lounge and Dining Room with gourmet food prepared by two Swiss chefs, plus the Last Run, the resort's night spot. The Kootenay Haus at the top of the Rosa run is a rustic log building containing a cafeteria and washrooms. It's a good place to hang out after the long ride up the T-bar. The Edelweiss restaurant is located in the Rocky Mountain Condominium Hotel just below the base area. There are also a number of restaurants in downtown Kimberley that are worth trying out. Just walk along the Platzl, and you'll pass a few of them and can decide. For a cappuccino and dessert, stop in at the Snowdrift Cafe in the Platzl. The InfoCentre on Wallinger Avenue has a full list of restaurants.

Most of the accommodation up at the ski resort is either condominiums or townhouses. The lodgings can house 1,200 guests and all are located just below the base of the ski area only a few minutes walk from the lifts. The Indoor Racquet Centre is located down here and has two tennis courts under bubbles as well as racquetball and wallyball. Equipment rentals are available. For reservation information call (604)427-5385 or the toll free reservations line, December to March: 1-800-663-4755. There are many other hotels and motels in Kimberley. Contact the InfoCentre, Box 63, Kimberley, B.C., V1Y 2Y5, for a complete listing.

Kimberley Ski and Summer Resort is one of the best family resorts in British Columbia. It offers a wide variety of ski terrain for all abilities, a good activities program, on-hill accommodation and the indoor racquet centre. These facilities will keep everyone in your group entertained for the length of your visit.

# PANORAMA

Box 7000
Invermere, B.C.
V0A 1K0

Reservations Toll Free: 1-800-663-2929
Information: (604)342-6941
In Toronto Call: (416)923-3838

**A** *Silver Platter*     **D** *Toby Chair*     **F** *Horizon Chair*
**B** *Red Rider*          **E** *Sunbird Chair*  **G** *Champagne T-bar*
**C** *Quad Chair*

**How To Get There**: By Car: Look for signs along Hwy 93 at Invermere in southeastern B.C. Panorama is 18 km west of Invermere and 3 hours from Calgary, Alberta.
By Air: Calgary International Airport — 3 hours by car; Cranbrook Airport — 2 hours away; Fairmont/Panorama Airport — 35 minutes away. Airport transfers are available by VIP coach.

*Panorama Ridge.*

Panorama is the Albertans' playground. It's just two hours southwest of Banff on Hwy 93 near Invermere, so most of the license plates in the parking lot are from Wild Rose Country. It's a self-contained, low-key family resort without the crowds of the more popular ski hills on the other side of the mountains. Surprisingly enough, at 1,162 m (3,800 ft.), Panorama has the longest vertical drop in the Canadian Rockies. It also has a milder climate than Banff and Lake Louise, averaging only -5° C throughout the winter months. Panorama doesn't receive as much snow, but with snowmaking on 60 per cent of the mountain, they can guarantee a long season.

The mountain was designed for intermediate skiers and those who love to cruise. Wide-open fall-line runs streak the face of the hill in a regular rhythm of unremarkable sameness which offers few skiing surprises. Luckily, Panorama also has many alternative activities to interest you. Every day has a full itinerary, usually starting mid-afternoon. Participate in cross-country ski tours, snowboard clinics or water-colour workshops offered during the week. Bring your skates along and take a few spins around the rink. Strap on some cross country skis and tour along the 22 km of track adjacent to the village. While you're in the neighbourhood, arrange to go for a horse-drawn sleigh ride. There is also a weight room, seven hot tubs, a hair salon, and massage therapy to straighten out any misaligned muscles.

To relax, play a game of darts in the Olde-English-style Strathcona pub located above the Horsethief Lodge reception. If you're feeling more energetic, try dancing at the Glacier Nightclub. The T-Bar & Grill, in the Pine Inn Hotel at the base of the quad chair, is licensed and serves food throughout the day. Try the Macho Natchos — they layer the cheese and chips and load on the jalepeño peppers. Guaranteed to warm you up. Shoot a game of pool while listening to live entertainment Thursday to Monday. The T-Bar & Grill also takes care of late night snacks by serving pizza from 9 p.m. to midnight.

There are several other restaurants at the resort. For those quiet, candlelit nights, the Toby Dining Room is the spot. It serves French and Californian cuisine at reasonable prices. The Starbird Dining Room takes care of families for breakfast, lunch and dinner. A large room facing the hill, it accommodates lots of folks and features daily specials.

Inn The Beginning is a basic cafeteria serving basic junk food. It's a good place to warm up your feet and grab a hot chocolate, but if you're here for the week, consider packing your own lunch. A small grocery store at the hill sells items like milk, cereals, condiments and some vegetables but is fairly limited so bring food with you.

The town of Invermere is just 18 km down the road, but once the car is parked, it seems hard to drive anywhere. Make the effort though. Invermere is a quaint little town that really hops in the summer. The Lakeside Pub at Athalmer Beach is a year-round gathering spot for the locals and tourists alike. It could have something to do with the incredible burgers and homemade fries they serve. If you've got a two-dollar bill you don't mind parting with, maybe you can add it to the collection on the walls.

There is accommodation in Invermere, but most people do stay right up at the ski hill. At the ski base, the Horsethief Lodge and Toby Creek Lodge are condominium units and the Pine Inn offers hotel rooms. The mountain lifts are easily accessible from all accommodation.

Another option for lodging is the Delphine Lodge, a beautiful bed and breakfast located in Wilmer just off the road to Panorama. Built in 1899, it has been completely renovated and decorated in old country charm. A tasty breakfast of home-baked goodies greets you after a sound night's sleep under a heavy down comforter. They're open year-round and can be reached at (604)342-6851. Panorama is only a ten-minute drive away.

Let's wind back up the road and go skiing. The 1989-90 season was a big year for Panorama. A new high-speed quad chair, nicknamed Quadzilla, whisks skiers half way up the mountain from the base lodge area. From here you can ski some beginner terrain off to the left or head for more advanced runs to the right, serviced by the Sunbird Chair. The Horizon Chair, a traditional double, takes over where the quad ends and carries you up to the top ridge line. This area is a little tougher, but there are a couple of wide-open cruising runs, Skyline and Rollercoaster, that will ease you down.

At the top of the Horizon Chair, the Champagne T-bar pokes further up the ridge and accesses black diamonds only. Champagne Chute, Top of the World and Picture Perfect, are narrow, bumpy and steep, and take you back to the T-bar. Schober's Dream, to the right, is a top-to-bottom, thigh-busting black diamond run to the Sunbird Chair.

The first-time skiers and kids have their own area and lifts. If you feel you're a little too old to ski through Big Bird and friends in the play area beside the Red Rider tow, the Silver Platter off to the left is another good beginner's slope.

For the toddlers, aged 18 months and up, the Kiddies Korral is open from 9 a.m. to 4 p.m. and includes toys, games, arts and crafts and snacks. They charge a nominal hourly rate and family discounts are available.

The popular Adventure Club Ski Program entertains the 6 to 12 year olds and runs from 10 a.m. to 3:30 p.m. It's a four-day package, and the price includes lunch, five hours of supervised ski lessons, games and arts and crafts. All classes are split according to age and ability. The Mountain Ski Week is a four-day program for adults and teens, offering lessons and a good way to meet new people.

*here's a great view around every corner at Panorama.*

Powder Performance gets you ready to ski the deep white stuff when you go heli-skiing with Heli-ski Panorama located just across Toby Creek from the resort. A two-day comprehensive clinic, video analysis and new Sybervision training prepare you for the experience. Sybervision involves watching videos of experts doing the proper moves which you incorporate into your mind's eye and use to improve your technique.

Don't envision the steep runs and deep powder of those wild extreme skiing movies when flying with Heli-Ski Panorama. They cater to first-time heli-skiers and those who wish a "no pressure" pace. They also offer the Powder Academy for novice powder skiers. Contact (604)342-6494.

Panorama Resort caters to everyone in the family and takes the worries out of a vacation. Ski-to-the-door accommodation, organized events and the longest vertical drop in the Canadian Rockies will keep everyone interested and entertained.

# PANORAMA

**Vertical Rise:** 1,162 m/ 3,800 ft.

**Elevations:** Base 1,036 m/ 3,400 ft.
Top 2,194 m/ 7,200 ft.

**Lifts:** Length
Silver Platter 480 m/ 1,600 ft.
Red Rider 185 m/ 500 ft.
Quad Chair 1,490 m/ 4,900 ft.
Toby Chair 585 m/ 1,900 ft.
Sunbird Chair 1,217 m /4,000 ft.
Horizon Chair 1,410 m /4,700 ft.
Champagne T-Bar 720 m /2,400 ft.

**Lift Capacity:** 6,800 skiers per hour

**Terrain Breakdown:** 20% Beginner
60% Intermediate
20% Advanced

**Total Terrain:** 300 acres

**Snowmaking:** 60% of terrain

**Average Temperature:** -5° C

**Number of Runs:** 33

**Season Dates:** December — late April

**Hours of Operation:** 9:00 - 4:00
Resort open year-round

**Facilities:** On-slope accommodation includes 255 condos and 102 hotel rooms, timeshare operation, daycare with organized indoor and outdoor activity programs, Kid's Adventure Club, day lodge, cafeteria, two dining rooms, six lounges/bars, general store, ski school, ski rentals, ski repairs, gift and sportswear retail outlets, saunas, hot tubs, massage therapist, exercise room, beauty salon, horse drawn sleigh rides and hayrides, ice skating, conference facilities, cross-country skiing (22km).

| 1990/91 Prices | Full Day | Half Day | 3 Day | 5 Day |
|---|---|---|---|---|
| Adult | $30 | $24 | $87 | $136 |
| Youth (5-14) | $18 | $15 | $52 | $75 |
| Child (Under 5) | FREE | | | |
| Seniors (65+) | $18 | $15 | | |

# WHITETOOTH SKI AREA

Box 1925
Golden, B.C.
V0A 1H0

Information: (604)344-6114
Accommodation: (604)344-7125

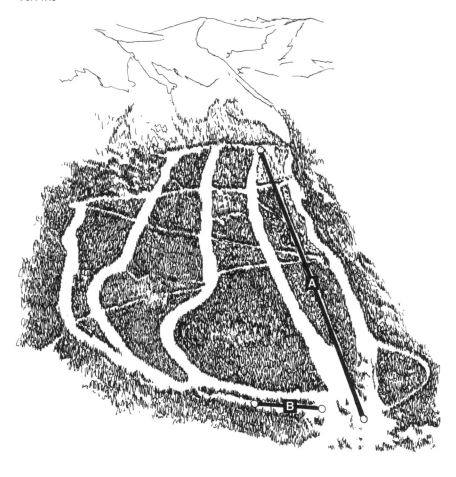

**A** *Pioneer Chair*    **B** *Blaeberry Handle Tow*

**How To Get There**: Whitetooth is located just 20 minutes from downtown Golden at the junction of Highway 95 and Highway 1. A ski bus picks up passengers at Golden Hardware at 8:30 a.m. and returns at 4:45 p.m.

## WHITETOOTH

|  |  |
|---|---|
| **Vertical:** | 530 m/ 1,740 ft. |
| **Elevations:** | Base 1,310 m/ 4,000 ft. |
| | Top 1,840 m/ 6,040 ft. |
| **Lifts:** | |
| Pioneer Double Chair | 530 m/ 1,740 ft. |
| Blaeberry Handle Tow | 183 m/ 600 ft. |
| **Terrain Breakdown:** | 33% Beginner |
| | 33% Intermediate |
| | 33% Advanced |
| **Average Temperature:** | -5° C |
| **Number of Runs:** | 9 |
| **Facilities:** | Day lodge, ski shop, rentals, cafeteria and ski school |
| **Season Dates:** | Mid-December to mid-April |
| **Hours of Operation:** | 9 a.m. - 3:30 p.m early season |
| | 9 a.m. - 4:00 p.m. after Feb.1 |
| | Friday, Saturday, Sunday, Monday and Holidays |

| 1990/91 Prices*: | Full Day | Half Day |
|---|---|---|
| Adult | $22 | $16 |
| Youth (13-18) | $16 | $12 |
| Child (6-12) | $10 | $8 |
| Under 6/ Over 60 | $3 | |

*Season's pass available.*

Whitetooth ski hill at Golden is located just east of the Roger's Pass snowbelt in the Purcell Mountains, the mountains reknowned for their powder. Usually skiers need to hire a helicopter to reach that beautiful snow but Whitetooth makes it all easier.

It's a small community hill owned by the regional district and operated by the Whitetooth Ski Society. Most of the skiers come from the Golden area so it feels comfortable and friendly, almost like a family, when you visit the hill. Everyone gathers in the Dogtooth Lodge, a cozy, log day lodge which houses a restaurant, ski school, ski patrol and rentals. A daycare is planned, as well.

The ski hill has nine runs divided evenly between beginner, intermediate and advanced. The Pioneer double chair is the only chair to the top, providing 530 m (1,740 ft.) of vertical to skiers. The 10,000-foot-long beginners' slope, Big Bend, is a gentle switchback trail that is groomed to keep it nice and smooth. Advanced skiers will have had their eyes on the lift line run, Pioneer, on the way up and want to give it a go. It's narrow and challenging. Porcupine and Kicking Horse are fall line runs that will also test your skiing ability. If you feel like cruising, try Waitabit and Kinbasket.

The Blaeberry tow, a 600-foot handle tow, runs perpendicular to the Pioneer Chair at the bottom of the hill and is the perfect area for beginners and children. There's room for everyone at Whitetooth, and there's no such thing as a lift line.

There are six to eight kilometres of ungroomed cross country ski trails adjacent to the ski hill. Ski touring into the bowl behind Whitetooth is easy from the top of the Pioneer chair, and the Bugaboos are just beyond if you want to get into more extensive mountaineering.

Whitetooth would like to do some upgrading but has decided to avoid going into debt to do it. Their planning strategy depends on usage and a "pay-as-you-go" approach to expansion. This is a good philosophy because they provide a fun, affordable community hill, and it would be a shame to see Whitetooth lose its local nature.

Inexpensive accommodation is available in Golden because winter is their off season. The town buzzes in the summer with climbers and rafters but is a bit of a sleepy hollow the rest of the year. The one thing you have to do though is have a beer at the Mad Trapper's pub. It's a rustic log building with a lot of character.

In the winter most people just drive through Golden on the road to other places. If you're travelling to ski resorts in the Rockies, why not stop for a bit? Whitetooth isn't really a destination ski hill, but it's an enjoyable break along the way.

# Cariboo

*Cariboo country is known for its cross-country skiing.*

In skiing circles, when people think of the Cariboo region, they generally picture a cross-country skier schussing along the many kilometres of developed trails maintained by the abundant lodges that specialize in this sport. The town of 100 Mile House with its many resorts is world famous for its marathons and other competitions, while other places such as Lac La Jeune near Kamloops is a destination facility combining cross-country skiing with a small downhill ski area.

The Cariboo is cowboy country in B.C., and the raw feeling of the wild west is still alive in its towns and inhabitants. Although thousands of desperately hopeful gold seekers scrambled throughout the Cariboo at the turn of the century, today this beautiful plateau in the heart of British Columbia is sparsely populated — an advantage on the ski hills and cross-country tracks. Troll Mountain at Quesnel and Mt. Timothy near 100 Mile House offer good community hills with no frills but they do have a genuine enthusiasm for the sport and a true friendliness that can be lost at highly developed, fast-paced resorts elsewhere.

# MT. TIMOTHY

Mt. Timothy Ski Society
c/o Box 33
100 Mile House, B.C.
V0K 2E0

Information & Snow Phone: (604)396-4244

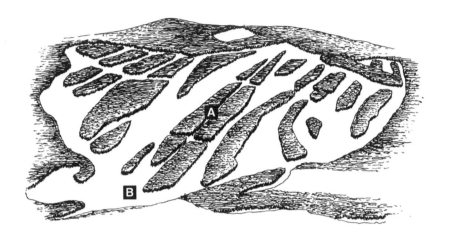

**A** *T-bar*  **B** *Handle Tow*

**How To Get There**: Driving north from 100 Mile House on Highway 97, take the east road at Lac La Hache. Mt. Timothy is 60 minutes from Williams Lake and 40 minutes from 100 Mile House. Bus trips are available from both towns, but should be confirmed by the snow phone for times and dates.

Mt. Timothy is predominantly a family mountain for beginning skiers with gentle terrain and wide, smooth, well-groomed runs. While not a destination ski hill, it is in the heart of the Cariboo's extensive nordic trails centred at 100 Mile House. If your family is split between cross country lovers and downhill fans, a visit to the area could satisfy everyone.

## MT. TIMOTHY

**Vertical Rise:** 260 m/ 850 ft.

**Elevations:** Base  1,375 m/ 4,510 ft.
Top   1,635 m/ 5,356 ft.

**Lifts:** T-bar (7 minute ride)
Handle Tow

**Lift Capacity:** 1,000 skiers per hour

**Terrain Breakdown:** 80% Beginner/ Intermediate
20% More Advanced

**Average Snowfall:** 2.5 m/ 7 - 8 ft.
1 - 1.5 m/ 3 - 4 ft. on ground

**Number of Runs:** 25

**Facilities:** Ski school, ski rentals, nordic skiing, new BR
400+ Bombardier groomer, new day lodge

**Season Dates:** Mid-December to mid-April
Open Friday to Monday but call snow phone
for up to date information.

**Hours of Operation:** 9 a.m. - 3:30 p.m.

**1989-90 Prices:**

| | |
|---|---|
| Adults | $16.00 |
| Youth (13 - 17) | $13.00 |
| Children (6 - 12) | $ 7.00 |
| Seniors & under 6 | FREE |

**Cross Country Trails\*:** 6 years to 65 years - $ 2.00

*includes map of trails*

Many special events happen during the season. The Coke "Go For Gold" Challenge takes place every weekend, and all are welcome to go for the gates. R.C.M.P. radar guns are put to good use in the "So You Think You're Fast" race, and during the Spring Break, test yourself on "Vertical Friday." The skier accumulating the most vertical distance wins.

There is a full-facility ski school with four full-time instructors. The handle tow is a good spot for the novice, and private and group rates are available. The new groomer provides consistently good ski conditions, making it even easier to learn at this user-friendly hill.

The ridge and slopes adjacent to the hill have been logged and are slated for a second T-bar. This will access some good terrain, including some advanced runs, and is about a third of the present area in size. These trails, like the others, all start at the top of the hill and take advantage of the full vertical drop which makes the runs seem reasonably long.

Nordic skiers can enjoy the 24 km (15 miles) of well-maintained trails nearby. There are up to 50 km of trails, but they are not all maintained on a regular basis. There is a small charge for the use of the nordic trails which includes a map. Telemark lessons are also available on request.

The nearest accommodation is in Timothy Lake, east of the hill turn-off or in Lac La Hache. There are also excellent facilities in 100 Mile House (see the Nordic Section, Cariboo-Chilcotin). For more information, contact the Cariboo Tourist Association at Box 4900, Williams Lake, B.C., V2G 2V8 or (604) 392-2226 or U.S. Toll Free 1-800-663-5885.

There is a strong sense of pride at Mt. Timothy, and the staff is friendly and tries to get to know everyone. It's a family-oriented mountain and the atmosphere creates the feeling of family. You're not a stranger when you arrive at Mt. Timothy, just a friend they don't know yet.

# TROLL SKI RESORT

Box 4013
Quesnel, B.C.
V2J 3J1

Information: (604)994-3373

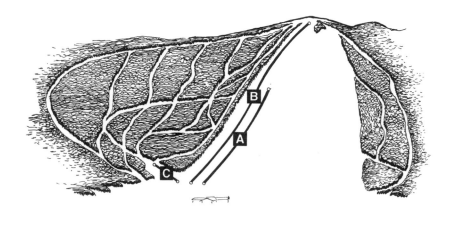

**A** *Blue T-bar*    **B** *Orange T-bar*    **C** *Yellow T-bar*

**How To Get There**: Troll is located 44 kilometres east of Quesnel on Highway 26. The cities of Quesnel and Williams Lake are serviced by air and B.C. Rail has both passenger service and ski packages to the Cariboo.

Troll Mountain's owner/operator Lars Fossberg tells the story of the ski hill's first day in December 1970, when 8 skiers turned out to try the T-bar at the new ski hill. They only had a log cabin and two outhouses, no telephone or hydro. Things have changed since then, and now Troll Mountain has 3 T-bars with another one under construction and even indoor plumbing. One thing hasn't changed though: the abundance of powder snow.

Troll is popular with locals and school groups who enjoy the friendly atmosphere, the powder, the variety of runs and the tree skiing. There is an excellent learning area with very gentle terrain and a vertical rise of only 33 m (120 ft.) off to the side of the lodge. The Blue and Orange T-bars rise parallel from the lodge up Troll Face, with the Blue T-bar stopping half way and the Orange reaching the top of the 1,528 m (5,000 ft.) peak. At almost two kilometres, the Orange T-bar is one of the longest in North America. A new T-bar for the 1990/91 season adds 92 m (300 ft.) of vertical to the hill.

The bulk of the trails are off to the left of the Orange T-bar. A long, beginner run called Snow White (the runs are named after those seven short guys and company) winds down the ridge and around the outside of the rest of the runs. Closer to the T-bar are a couple of black diamonds and some intermediate pitches accessed from Snow White. In mid-winter, you'll enjoy exploring the tree areas.

You'll want to enjoy the festivities at the hill because there's little to offer for night life in Quesnel. The Valhalla Restaurant has a wide-ranging menu so something will have to sound interesting. Lars recommends the Green Leaf Chinese restaurant. You can also look east to historic Wells and Barkerville for accommodation.

Troll Mountain will cater to private parties and larger groups for day lodge rental and night skiing, just phone ahead to arrange it.

This is a family-run and family-oriented ski hill that has good snow and a good atmosphere. It's not a destination resort, but like Mt. Timothy in the south Cariboo, it's in a great cross country skiing area. Try combining the two sports and see if you can't double your fun.

## TROLL SKI RESORT

**Vertical Rise**: 460 m/ 1,500 ft.

**Elevations**: Base 925 m/ 3,000 ft.
Top 1,388 m/ 4,510 ft.

| **Lifts**: | Vertical | Length |
|---|---|---|
| Blue T-bar | 209 m/ 680 ft. | 770 m/ 2,500 ft. |
| Orange T-bar | 460 m/ 1,500 ft. | 2,000 m/ 6,500 ft. |
| Yellow T-bar | 33 m/ 120 ft. | |

**Terrain Breakdown**: 25% Beginner
50% Intermediate
25% Advanced

**Total Terrain**: 220 acres of groomed runs

**Average Temperature**: -10° C January/ February

**Average Snowfall**: 1 - 2 m/ 3 - 6 ft.
Average Base 1 m/ 3 ft.

**Number of Runs**: 13

**Facilities**: Ski school, ski shop, ski patrol, day lodge, ski rentals, cafeteria with beer & wine license.

**Season Dates**: December to mid April

**Hours of Operation**: 9:00 - 3:30 p.m.
Night Skiing - Phone for hours or CKCQ Radio 920 in Quesnel.

| **1990/91 Prices** | Full Day | Half Day |
|---|---|---|
| Adults | $19 | $14 |
| Youth (7-17) | $14 | $10 |
| Child (Under 7) | FREE | |
| Seniors | $9.50 | $7 |

**Yellow T-Bar Only***:

| | | |
|---|---|---|
| Full Day (age 7 +) | $8 | |
| Night Skiing (Wed.) | $7 | |

*includes one run on the Blue or Orange T-bar

# North Country

*Fun for all ages is assured at the family-oriented resorts in B.C.'s North Country.*

Northern B.C. is a land of rugged mountains, long winters and cold weather, but these northern communities know how to make good use of those snowy winter months and, like in southern B.C., almost every town has its own ski hill. Many are small, local hills catering to the surrounding population, like Murray Ridge at Fort St. James, but some, like Powder King in Mackenzie and Hudson Bay Mountain in Smithers, are full destination resorts.

# MURRAY RIDGE SKI AREA

Box 866
Fort St. James, B.C.
V0J 1P0

Information: (604)996-8513

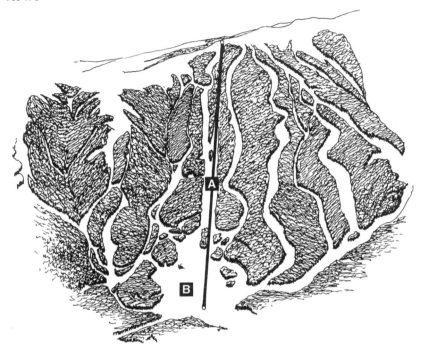

**A** *Dopplemayr T-bar*    **B** *Beginner Tow*

**How To Get There**: Murray Ridge is located 16 km north of Fort St. James on Highway 27 north of Vanderhoof and 100 km north west of Prince George.

Fort St. James is nestled on the south east shores of Stuart Lake. With about 2,300 residents, it's a quiet town of spectacular scenery and with a long history. Established by Simon Fraser in 1806 as a Northwest/Hudson's Bay Company Trading Post, Fort St. James was the centre of commerce and headquarters for the New Caledonia District, which included almost all of what became the central interior of B.C. The trading post has been restored to the 1890s period and is part of the Fort St. James National Historic Park.

Murray Ridge ski area is located 16 km north of town. It was first developed in 1975 and in 1980 the 2 km (6,500 ft.) T-bar,

*Skiers enjoy Murray Ridge's run variety.*

one of the longest in North America, was installed. There is a wide variety of terrain for every level of skier on over 32 km (20 miles) of runs.

It's fairly easy to find an area to suit your ability at the hill. From the top of the t-bar, ski right for beginner and intermediate runs and off to the left for two long ridge and gully lines rated as black diamond. A tow is located in the wide open area just up from the lodge for beginners and children. There are gentle, long runs like Middle River and Apollo to ski from the top.

The Ridge is operated by a board of local residents who ensure that the original idea of providing the community with family recreation is maintained. The support of the community is overwhelming, and the entire ski area has been built by local efforts. In 1986, a 10,000-square-foot day lodge was built which offers a licensed cafeteria, a 120-seat licensed lounge, ski tuning and rental shop and locker rentals. It also has a spectacular view of the mountains.

Murray Ridge Nordic Ski Club was formed in 1989 and will look toward further development of the cross country trails at the base of the alpine hill. The terrain in the wilderness areas around Fort St. James provides the nordic skier and winter camper with some great skiing and scenery.

Each February, Murray Ridge Ski Hill hosts the Great Bathtub Race. It is definitely something you have to see to believe. An amazing amount of imagination and work goes into creating the outrageous bathtubs on skis that challenge a downhill obstacle course. With one daring rider and three skiers per bathtub trying to maneuver through a course that includes a small jump, the spectators are treated to hilarious antics.

Fort St. James and Murray Ridge are a little out of the way for most skiers, but if you happen to find yourself in the area, make sure to drop in. The hill has a laid back, relaxed atmosphere that will have you feeling like one of the family in no time.

## MURRAY RIDGE

**Vertical:** 520 m/ 1,700 ft.

**Elevations:** Base 700 m/ 2,300 ft.
Top 1,220 m/ 4,000 ft.

**Lifts:** Length
Dopplemayr T-bar 1,980 m/ 6,500 ft.
Beginner Tow 213 m/ 700 ft.

**Terrain Breakdown:** 25% Beginner
25% Intermediate
50% Advanced

**Number of Runs:** 19

**Facilities:** 10,000-sq.-ft. day lodge, Licensed cafeteria, licensed lounge, lockers, ski rentals and tuning.

**Season Dates:** Mid-December to mid-April

**Hours of Operation:** Friday, Saturday, Sunday & Monday
Open during Christmas holidays (except Christmas Day), New Year's and Easter.
Weekdays: 10 a.m. to 4 p.m.
Weekends: 9:30 a.m. to 4 p.m.

**Cross-country trails:** 14 km of groomed trails

**Annual Events:** Mid February - The Great Bathtub Race
Mid March - Beach Party Weekend

**1989/90 Rates:**

| | |
|---|---|
| Adults | $17 |
| Student (with card) | $13 |
| Children 7 to 12 | $9 |
| Under 6/Over 65 | FREE |

# POWDER KING

Powder King Ski Village
Box 2405
Mackenzie, B.C.
V0J 2C0

Snow Phone & Info Centre: (604)561-1776 (Prince George)
Reservations: 1-800-663-8207

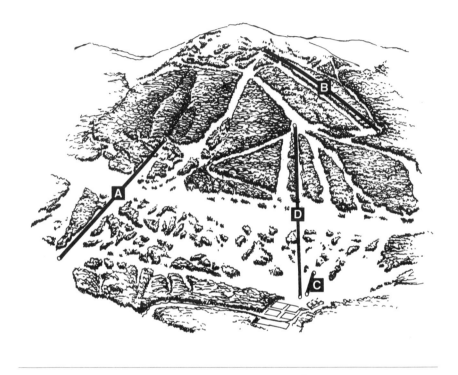

**A** *T-bar*  **C** *Platter Tow*  **D** *Powder Chair*
**B** *Alpine T-bar*

**How To Get There**: Powder King is located in Pine Pass on Hart Highway #97, 203 km (122 miles) north of Prince George. Fly into Dawson Creek or Prince George, rent a car, take a bus or drive all the way. Ski buses from Prince George run on the weekends and holidays only, call for information.

Powder King lives up to its name. An average of 12.5 metres of snow falls on this northern ski hill every winter. The cooler temperatures and high base elevation provide the perfect velvety snow that makes skiing so easy and enjoyable.

You may remember this ski hill by its original name, Azu. It was purchased in 1979 and renamed Powder King. The new owners saw development potential on the other side of the mountain and moved the base facilities half a mile away to the present location. The old Azu cafe is still used for staff accommodation.

The powder and tree skiing are what make Powder King memorable. The only problem can be finding terrain that is steep enough to ski with all that snow. Most of the runs are rated for intermediate skiers and provide great cruising for those not ready or willing to ski in the trees. Satisfaction, a steep, fall-line run from the top of the Alpine T-bar, will also provide plenty of challenge on those deep days.

*There's plenty of powder at Powder King.*

The lower T-bar accesses a side of the mountain that sees less use than the triple chair and alpine T-bar. This area is good for beginners and intermediates who want to concentrate and challenge themselves without having to worry about excessive traffic or surprises. A platter next to the triple chair is perfect for beginners and children.

The mountain expansion planned for Azu and North Eastern bowls will help spread out the skiers, and more expert terrain is planned in the immediate future with runs cut in the Roller Coaster and old Azu area. Powder King is rarely crowded, but these new areas will offer exciting, untouched skiing for everybody.

Powder King has a comprehensive ski school program. They offer first time rental/lesson packages at rock bottom prices, group and private lessons plus ski improvement workshops for the intermediate and advanced skiers who get to pick their own terrain. The Powder Pups program, for kids seven and under, is a fun session designed for children to ski with others of similar ability. Three- and five-lesson packages are available. If you don't want a lesson, but don't know the mountain either, the Powder King Ski Friends will help you get the most out of your ski day.

Powder King prides itself on being comfortable, unpretentious and friendly. The 60 on-hill rooms at the Village Beds are just that; nothing fancy, and certainly not expensive, but you will definitely be comfortable. There's even an outdoor hot tub, open from 10 a.m. to 10 p.m. If you want to be a little more active, the King's Tavern is the spot for apres-ski entertainment with a fully licensed room, snacks and video games. There is also a family entertainment centre with video machines, pool table and movies to keep skiers of all ages interested. The Azu Mountain Cafe is a fully licensed dining room offering fine dining in a comfortable atmosphere.

Powder King will be undergoing some expansion in the next few years. A hotel/commercial complex will be the first stage of development, followed by tennis courts, condotels, summer activities as well as more lift capacity and more runs to raise the total daily skier maximum from 2,000 to 5,000 per day.

Every weekend sees a different event planned. In mid-February, the Half Way to Summer Bash and Boogie hosts an air band contest with best costume prizes. The first weekend in April is Powder King's anniversary so watch out for Azu Antics and more great costumes. On-going throughout the season are 2-for-1 Tuesdays, movie nights, bonfires, volleyball and more. Though Powder King is far removed from the crowds, it really knows how to entertain the people that do make the trip.

As they say up there, Powder King is the place to go for guaranteed snow. Add that to the continual events happening at the hill, and you're bound to have a great time.

# POWDER KING

**Vertical:** 640 m/ 2,100 ft.

**Elevations:** Base 944 m/ 3,500 ft.
Top 1,834 m/ 6,019 ft.

| **Lifts:** | Vertical |
|---|---|
| T-bar | |
| Platter | |
| Powder Triple Chair | 387 m/ 1,270 ft. |
| Alpine T-bar | 255 m/ 829 ft. |

**Lift Capacity:** 2,000 skiers per hour

**Terrain Breakdown:** 35% Beginner
40% Intermediate
25% Advanced

**Total Terrain:** 453 acres

**Average Temperature:** -12°C

**Average Snowfall:** 12.5m/ 495 in.

**Number of Runs:** 18 + gladed runs

**Facilities:** 60 room on-hill hotel, two licensed restaurants, pub, ski school, ski rentals, ski shop, repairs, childminding, cafeteria, RV parking.

**Season Dates:** Mid-November to late April

| **Hours of Operation:** | Dec. 1 - Mar. 9 | Mar. 10 - April 30 |
|---|---|---|
| Weekdays | 9:30 a.m.-3:30 p.m. | 9:30 a.m.-4:00 p.m. |
| Weekends | 9:00 a.m.-3:30 p.m. | 9:00 a.m.-4:00 p.m. |

| **1990/91 Prices:** | Full Day | Half Day |
|---|---|---|
| Adult | $28 | $22 |
| Youth (13-17) | $22 | $17 |
| Child (8-12) | $17 | $14 |
| Senior/Under 8 | FREE | |
| Powder Pups lessons* | $10/ hr. | |

**Ski 'n' Stay**:**

| 2 day/ 1 night*** | $65 |
|---|---|
| 2 day/ 2 night | $82 |
| 3 day/ 2 night | $106 |
| 4 day/ 3 night | $147 |
| 5 day/ 4 night | $188 |

*half day program introduced in 1991/92

**per person based on double occupancy.

***not available on Friday or Saturday

# SKI SMITHERS

Smithers Ski Corporation
Box 492
Smithers, B.C.
V0J 2N0

Information: (604) 847-2058
Toll Free (B.C.): 1-800-665-4299

**A** *Triple Chair*        **C** *Green T-bar*        **D** *Beginner Tow*
**B** *Orange T-bar*

**How To Get There**: Smithers is on Highway 16 in northwestern B.C. and Hudson Bay Mountain is 22 km (14 miles) west of town. There are daily flights to Smithers from Vancouver via Canadian Airlines and daily flights from Terrace and Prince George via Central Mountain Air. Greyhound Bus Lines offers daily service from points east and west. Daily ski bus service to the mountain is available from most lodging facilities in Smithers.

Skiers in northern B.C. and the Alaskan Panhandle have discovered a ski hill that has plenty of light, dry powder and a welcoming, family atmosphere. Hudson Bay Mountain at Smithers is the place that these northern skiers have been keeping under their toques. But the word is out. Back in the 1920s, a group of friends and winter enthusiasts formed the Smithers Ski Club. They cleared the trees for the first ski run and installed the first rope tow on Hudson Bay Mountain. Over the years, this group explored and developed "The Mountain," as its known among locals, and in 1980, together with the town of Smithers, created the Smithers Ski Corporation. Now there are three lifts reaching to the top of the mountain and a beginner's tow near the Upper Chalet. It's come a long way from the days of lugging homemade skis up to the peak and camping overnight in the tiny log cabin built among the trees.

The ski hill has gained the attention of northern skiers for a number of reasons. Part of the attraction is the friendly attitude at the mountain. There aren't many hills around where a guest book is left out for first time visitors to the area to leave behind their impressions. You'll also notice that there are lots of children and seniors around. They do get to ski for free here, but more than that, skiing is a family activity in Smithers. Ultimately though, it's the snow and the terrain that keeps them coming back again and again.

The dry, cold snow that isn't found on the coast, the vertical, the lack of crowds and the tree skiing are the secrets of to Smithers' popularity. For all that powder, they can thank a

*Dry, cold snow makes Smithers a great powder area.*

low pressure system that sits in the Gulf of Alaska and sends moisture-laden clouds southwest over the coastal mountains into the cooler, inland regions. Here the moisture falls as snow on the higher peaks, like Hudson Bay Mountain, whose glaciers cool the air and dry the snow even further.

Don't be fooled by cloudy, cold and foggy days in the valley. Often it's only a weather phenomenon called a low-level inversion which traps the colder air under it and, above the cap, the temperatures can be 10 to 15 degrees warmer with sunny skies. Anytime you see the smoke from the sawmill fan out instead of going up, you know there's an inversion. Grab your skis and get up there.

On the mountain there is a run for every level of ability, so you're sure to find something you like. The novice runs around the Green T-bar, called the Cabin Runs and the Nancy Greene run, are the original ski area from almost 20 years ago. They are short, the tow doesn't take too long, and there are no moguls or fast skiers to watch out for.

The Orange T-bar has a wide variety of runs, with most of the advanced pitches the mountain has to offer. Try waiting until afternoon when the sun has had a chance to soften the snow up before testing yourself on these slopes.

The Triple Chair, down by the lower chalet, services the big, cruising runs on the mountain, interspersed with a few challenging black diamonds. Ptarmigan is a good morning warm-up run when it's been freshly groomed and try out Alpenhorn for its challenge and its views. You can look out over the valley and not see the bottom — yes, it's steep. Footloose is an intermediate run that is left ungroomed so it's a good spot to learn how to ski bumps.

One thing about the layout of the hill is that you have to pay attention to your timing at the end of the day if you want to get back to the parking lots without considerable effort. Sidewinder is useful for getting back to the lower parking lot once the T-bar has shut down. Another option is to switch at the top of the Orange T-bar and go down Panorama to the Blue Chair.

Over the past few years, Ski Smithers has redesigned their children's programs, giving consideration to the younger child's undeveloped muscle control, endurance and social skills. Kinderkamp is for the young ones who haven't skied before and offers a one-hour lesson and childminding for the day. Ski-wee group lessons are for ages three to seven who have had some experience on skis. Private lessons are available to all skiers, even preschoolers.

It seems like the cross country skiing opportunities are endless around Smithers and Telkwa, a community just to the south. Trail building on the Smithers Community Forest adjacent to the popular Pine Creek trails has greatly expanded skiing on the set tracks. There are more than a dozen other areas for nordic skiing, ranging from the Smithers Golf Course and Tyee Lake Provincial Park to more strenuous trails up old mining and logging roads throughout the Bulkley Valley.

Day trips for backcountry ski tours are a bit limited around Smithers but there are great overnight trips. An easily accessible route to the alpine is only a short distance from Hudson Bay Mountain. Just ride up the Green T-bar and head out across the flats, known as the Prairie, for a couple of kilometres to Crater Lake. The Ski Smithers staff can give you directions.

The Babine Recreation Area directly across the valley has some easily accessed routes up Driftwood Canyon, including Harvey Mountain, and a longer ski up to Silver King Basin. There are many more areas to explore around the valley. For more information on touring around here, call the district parks office at (604)847-7320.

Smithers and Hudson Bay Mountain may seem a little remote for the Lower Mainland skier. But for the people in the north, the excellent ski and snow conditions, friendly atmosphere and uncrowded slopes of this ski hill make the long, cold winters easier to bear.

# SKI SMITHERS

**Vertical:** 525 m/ 1,750 ft.

**Elevations:** Base 1,126 m/ 3,750 ft.
Top 1,650 m/ 5,500 ft.

**Lifts:** Length
Triple Chair Lift 1,836 m/ 6,022 ft.
Orange T-Bar 1,158 m/ 3,800 ft.
Green T-Bar 670 m/ 2,200 ft.
Beginner Tow 107 m/ 350 ft.

**Terrain Breakdown:** 25% Beginner
50% Intermediate
25% Advanced

**Average Temperature:** -12°C

**Average Snowfall:** 244 cm/ 96 in.

**Average Snow Base:** 145 cm/ 57 in.

**Number of Runs:** 18

**Facilities:** *The Upper Chalet:* licensed cafeteria, brown-bag lunch room, licensed lounge, Kids Korner, lockers.
*The Lower Chalet:* licensed snack bar, brown bag lunch room.
*Kids Korner:* offers childminding 7 days a week from 10 a.m. to 4 p.m. for children 3 to 8 years.
Ski rentals, lessons, ski tuning.

**Season Dates:** Mid-November to mid-April

**Hours of Operation:**
Midweek 10:00 a.m. - 4:00 p.m.
Weekends 9:30 a.m. - 4:00 p.m.
Holidays 9:30 a.m. - 4:00 p.m.

**Lift Schedule:** Triple Chair/ Orange T-bar open Monday to Friday.
Beginner Tow will operate during lesson times, on weekends and during holiday periods.
All lifts open Saturdays, Sundays and holiday periods except Christmas Day when only Orange T-bar open from 11:00 - 3:00 p.m.

| 1990/91 Prices | Full Day | Half Day | 3 Day | 5 Day |
|---|---|---|---|---|
| Adult | $27 | $19 | $69 | $110 |
| Youth (8-12) | $13 | $11 | $48 | $75 |
| Child (Under 8) | FREE | | | |
| Seniors | FREE | | | |

# High Country

*Tod Mountain, near Kamloops.*

Mt. Mackenzie at Revelstoke and Tod Mountain near Kamloops are both gearing up for substantial development of their ski hills and resorts, building on solid bases of good terrain and snow conditions. Tod Mountain also benefits from the Coquihalla Highway, which makes it a much shorter, easier drive from the Lower Mainland.

# HARPER MOUNTAIN

Harper Mountain Ski Lifts Ltd.
2042 Valleyview Drive
Kamloops, B.C.
V2C 4C5

Office: (604)372-2119
Lodge: (604)573-5115
Ski School & Shop: (604)573-4040 or (604)374-0448

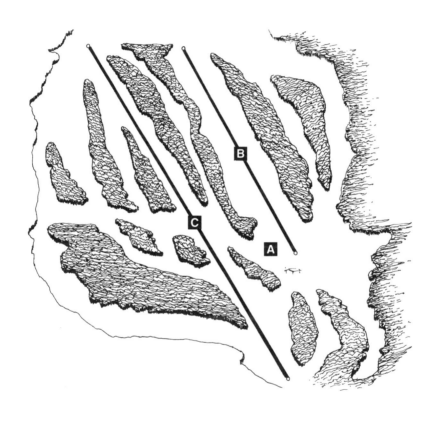

**A** *Handle Tow*          **B** *Big T-bar*          **C** *Huser Chair*

**How To Get There**: Harper Mountain, overlooking Paul Lake, is 23 km northeast of Kamloops. Take Hwy 5 north from Kamloops and watch for signs.

## HARPER MOUNTAIN

**Vertical**: 425 m/ 1,394 ft.

**Elevations**: Daylodge: 1,220 m/ 4,002 ft.
Peak: 1,520 m/ 4,987 ft.

| **Lifts**: | Vertical | Length |
|---|---|---|
| Handle Tow | | |
| Big T-Bar | 210 m/ 689 ft. | 803 m/ 2634 ft. |
| Huser Triple Chair | 425 m/ 1394 ft. | 1376 m/ 4515 ft. |

**Terrain Breakdown**: 25% Beginner
50% Intermediate
25% Advanced

**Number of Runs**: 13

**Facilities**: Daylodge, licensed cafeteria, rental shop, ski school
Cross country trails - 13 km
Limited snowmaking

**Season Dates**: Mid-December to end of March (snow permitting)

**Hours of Operation**: Daily Operation 9:30 a.m. to 4 p.m.
Night Skiing
Wed., Thurs., Fri., 6 - 10 p.m.
Mid Week - T-bar & Handle Tow all day with triple chair after 12:30 p.m.

| **1990/91 Prices**: | Full Day | Half day | Night |
|---|---|---|---|
| Adult (15+) | $19.00 | $13.50 | $11.00 |
| Youth (6-14) | $14.50 | $10.50 | $8.00 |
| Child (5 & Under) | FREE | | |
| Seniors | $14.50 | | |

| **T-bar/ Handle Tow** | Full Day | Half Day |
|---|---|---|
| Adult | $16.00 | $12.00 |
| Everyone Else | $12.00 | $9.00 |

Harper Mountain is an often-overlooked destination when skiing around Kamloops. Tod Mountain usually gets all the press. But Harper Mountain is ideally designed for the average skier and caters to many families from Kamloops and the surrounding area. It is a family-oriented and family-operated ski hill, and much of its popularity is due to the warm and congenial atmosphere which a smaller ski area can provide.

The north-facing slopes hold their snow long after it has disappeared in the valley, and limited snowmaking improves the coverage as well. A triple chair and T-bar both reach the peak of Harper Mountain and access a variety of runs. The pitches, under and on, both sides of the triple chair, such as Monashee, Cliffhanger and Bush Whacker are all black diamonds. The T-bar, which is lit for night skiing on Wednesdays, Thursdays and Fridays, offers a gentler selection.

A beautiful, log-framed day lodge with a floor-to-ceiling stone fireplace is the gathering place for skiers at Harper. There is a licensed cafeteria in the lodge along with a well-equipped rental shop and the ski school.

Harper Mountain ski school offers a number of specific programs for kids as they progress through the various stages of skiing. The handle tow in front of the lodge is the setting for these lessons, providing easy viewing for the parents. The Junior programs, for 8 - 14 year olds, start off with the Ski Dozers, followed by Snow Star and then Snow Jets. These packages include four two hour lessons, lift tickets and rentals. The Tiny Tot programs teach the 4 to 7 year olds in three different groups and include four one-hour lessons plus rental equipment for three hours.

Cross country skiers can leave from the day lodge and enjoy the 13 km of scenic trails overlooking the South Thompson Valley. There is no charge for use of the trails and they are not patrolled. Cross country ski rentals are available at the lodge.

# MT. MACKENZIE SKI AREA

Box 1000
Revelstoke, B.C.
V0E 2S0

Phone: (604)837-5268

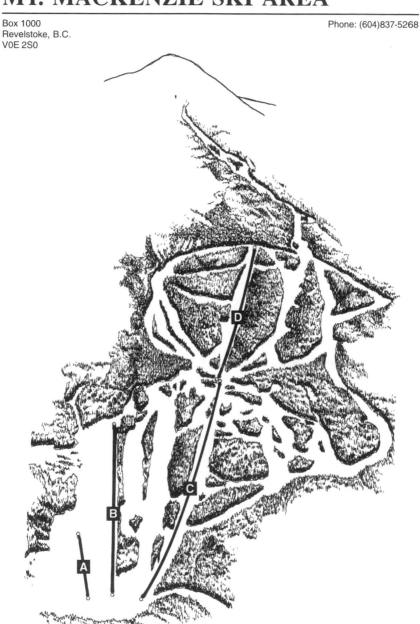

**A** *Choo Choo Handle Tow*  **C** *Selkirk Chair*  **D** *Monashee Chair*
**B** *Housetrack T-bar*

*Mt. Mackenzie lift lines are usually short.*

**How To Get There:** Revelstoke is located on the upper Columbia River, between the Rogers and Eagle Passes in the Selkirk Mountains on the Trans Canada Highway. Mount Mackenzie is just 6 km from downtown Revelstoke.

David Thompson and his crew were the first white men to come down the Columbia River and view this area in 1811. The short-lived Big Bend Gold Rush of the 1860s brought miners seeking their fortune. In the 1880s, the Canadian Pacific Railway drove the last spike in their trans-Canada line at Craigellachie, 28 miles west of Revelstoke, on November 7, 1885. Railroading has been the support of the economy for over one hundred years but tourism is becoming more important. The historic character of Revelstoke is evident in the quaint, well-kept Victorian houses spaced along the wide streets, with snowbanks built up past the windowsills.

Mount Mackenzie keeps you on your toes. Steep, narrow fall-line runs, sudden transitions and an expansive view of the Monashee Mountains across the valley will all absorb your attention. The ski hill is located in an area known for its heli-ski operations and for the quality, and quantity, of the snow. Currently only the bottom third of the mountain has been developed for skiing, but the hill is in the process of changing ownership and this should mean big changes so that in the next few years there may be lifts that reach to the top of the mountain and access all the snow that the alpine receives.

Mt. Mackenzie is serviced by the Selkirk and Monashee chairlifts which take you up 2,000 vertical feet, about one third of the way up the mountain. Mackenzie has a variety of trails with The Spike, off to the left of the Monashee chair, being the toughest. All runs are basically the same layout: relatively narrow, fall- line runs over rolling hills. The grooming leaves some interesting lumps and bumps to deal with so keep your eyes open.

## MT. MACKENZIE SKI AREA

**Vertical:** 614 m/ 2015 ft.

**Elevations:** Base 480 m/ 1575 ft.
Top 1094 m/ 3590 ft.

| Lifts: | Vertical | Length |
|---|---|---|
| Choo Choo Handle Tow | 47 m/ 155 ft. | 308 m/ 1,011 ft. |
| Housetrack T-Bar | 175 m/ 575 ft. | 751 m/ 2,465 ft. |
| Selkirk Double Chair | 310 m/ 1,017 ft. | 1,059 m/ 3,475 ft. |
| Monashee Double Chair | 295 m/ 968 ft. | 915 m/ 3,002 ft. |

**Lift Capacity:** 2,820 skiers per hour

**Terrain Breakdown:** 25% Beginner
50% Intermediate
25% Advanced

**Average Temperature:** -3° C (in the valley)

**Average Snowfall:** 460 cm/ 15 ft.

**Runs:** 21

**Facilities:** Cafeteria, Golden Spike Saloon, ski school, ski rentals, babysitting, nightskiing, heli & cat skiing, cross-country trails nearby, ski shop.

**Cat Skiing:** Cat Powder Skiing (604)837-9489.

**Season Dates:** Mid-December to late March

**Hours of Operation:** Weekdays 9 - 3:30
Tuesdays Closed
Weekends/ Holidays 9 - 3:30
Night Skiing Wed & Fri 6 - 10 p.m.

| 1989/90 Prices*: | T-bar Only | Weekends & Holidays | Mid Week |
|---|---|---|---|
| Full Day Adult | $13 | $20 | $18 |
| Junior (13-18 years) | $10 | $15 | $13 |
| Child (8-12 years) | $8 | $11 | $9 |
| Half Day** Adult | $10 | $14 | $12 |
| Junior | $8 | $10 | $9 |
| Child | $6 | $7 | $6 |
| Evening Adult | $10 | | |
| Junior | $8 | | |
| Child | $6 | | |

*Seniors - 50% discount*

*Special 3 or 5 day and group passes available*

**Half Day starts at 12:30 p.m.*

The Choo Choo handle tow and the Housetrack T-bar access a wide open beginner's area at the base. There are no direct runs entering from above so the beginners have the whole slope to themselves.

The Golden Spike Saloon has a great south-facing patio where the locals gather in the sunshine after skiing. The cafeteria serves the standard short-order menu with burgers and fries, salads and sandwiches.

The city of Revelstoke has numerous motels to stay at. Winter is the off season, so rates are quite reasonable. The restaurants available are a little bleak, but there are a couple worth mentioning. Emo's on 1st Avenue has a large menu serving Greek food, steaks and seafood. It's not too expensive and the portions are big. The other spot is Snuggles just off the main street. It's an old pink house that serves good home-made food that's not your standard interior town restaurant fare. The Little European Deli offers a tasty sandwich for a change from the cafeteria food at the hill.

Revelstoke is fairly quiet for night life, aside from the usual bars, but there are some other options. The Best Western Hotel across Highway 1 has a pool and you can buy a pass to go swimming. Also, the community centre has a weight room and jacuzzi that are open to the public. Check for available times. Don't forget that Mt. Mackenzie has night skiing on Wednesdays and Fridays from 6 p.m. to 10 p.m.

Cross country skiers can scoot up to Mount Revelstoke National Park and tour the five kilometre packed and groomed trail they maintain. Two kilometres are lit for night skiing. Skiers can also head up the Summit Road, beginning one kilometre from the Trans-Canada Highway.

Mount Revelstoke and Glacier national parks are both well known for some of the most challenging ski touring in Canada. Telemark and ski mountaineering equipment is far more practical than cross country gear for these areas. Anyone heading into the parks for a trip should check with the park wardens at Rogers Pass for Glacier and in Revelstoke for Mount Revelstoke on the requirements for registration. During the avalanche control season (November to the end of April), all slopes adjacent to the Trans-Canada Highway are closed to skiing.

Revelstoke and Mount Mackenzie are on the verge of a big step up in their ski area profile. With the sale of the hill, the expected new development will put the town on the ski map. Even now it's a tough little hill that demands your concentration. Lifts to the top and to the powder will round out the mountain.

# TOD MOUNTAIN

Box 869
Kamloops, B.C.
V2C 5M8

Information and Reservations: (604)372-5757
Snow Phone: (604)372-7224
Mountain Office Phone: (604)578-7222
Central Reservations: 1-800-663-2838

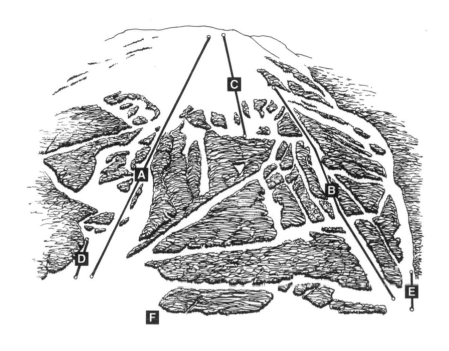

| | | |
|---|---|---|
| **A** *Burfield Chair* | **C** *Crystal Chair* | **E** *Handle Tow* |
| **B** *Shuswap Chair* | **D** *Big Platter* | **F** *Little Platter* |

**How To Get There**: Kamloops is only 3.5 hours from Vancouver via the Coquihalla freeway. To get to Tod Mountain, follow Highway 5 north from Kamloops to the Heffley Creek turn-off to the east. Tod Mountain is a half hour drive (27 km) up this paved road. Check for commercial flights into Kamloops airport.

Tod is a big mountain. Long intermediate runs from its bald dome or the short steep pitches above treeline will have your legs aching for a break. Beginners can ski from the top to the bottom on the wide and diverse 5-Mile run, and powder hounds will love those abundant deep days. Variety is the attraction at this fun mountain located 40 minutes north east of Kamloops.

After the scenic drive up the valley, you will arrive at the first of Tod's two base areas. At the lower Burfield base there is a new 45-room hotel and other hill facilities, including the usual retail, rental and ticket sales as well as overnight parking. The double Burfield Chair rises from here at the bottom to the top with a mid-station along the way, and what a long way it is. Another kilometre along the road is the upper Shuswap base where there is also a licensed day lodge, rental and retail shops, ski school, ski patrol and lift tickets. The Shuswap Chair reaches up about two thirds of the mountain. From there, you can ski over to connect with the Crystal Chair to the peak.

A perception about Tod is that there aren't very many runs for the absolute beginner. On the map, eight green slopes are marked but in reality, most blend into each other, and there is only one on the Crystal Chair at the top of the mountain. A beginner would probably be happy on the Big Platter Lift at the Shuswap base area. If they want to explore and push themselves more, they could try the Burfield Chair, skiing off to the right and following Cahilty along the boundary. The kids can join

*Tod Mountain.*

## TOD MOUNTAIN

**Vertical**: 945 m/ 3,100 ft.

**Elevations**: Burfield Base: 1,297 m/ 3,960 ft.
Shuswap Base: 1,225 m/ 4,020 ft.
Summit: 2,149 m/ 7,050 ft.

| Lifts: | Vertical | Length |
|---|---|---|
| Burfield Chair(double) | 934 m/ 3,064 ft. | 2,835 m/ 9,300 ft. |
| Shuswap Chair(double) | 610 m/ 2,000 ft. | 2,133 m/ 7,000 ft. |
| Crystal Chair(triple) | 282 m/ 926 ft. | 975 m/ 3,200 ft. |
| Big Platter Lift | 142 m/ 466 ft. | 380 m/ 1,246 ft. |
| Handle Tow | 3.6 m/ 12 ft. | 146 m/ 480 ft. |
| Little Platter Lift | 106 m/ 348 ft. | 480 m/ 1,576 ft. |

**Lift Capacity**: 4,790 skiers per hour

**Terrain Breakdown**: 19% Beginner & Low Intermediate
34% Intermediate
28% Advanced Intermediate
19% Advanced

**Total Terrain**: 330 acres

**Average Temperature**: -10°C

**Average Snowfall**: 680 cm/ 22 ft.

**Average Base**: 200 cm/ 6.5 ft.

**Number of Runs**: 46

**Facilities**: *Upper Base - Shuswap:* Licensed day lodge, rental shop, retail shop, ski school, parking, ski patrol, lift tickets.
*Lower Base - Burfield:* Day lodge bar (lounge), Bierstube, retail shop, rental shop, ski school, parking, overnight parking, lift tickets, information, bed & breakfast reservations.

**Season Dates**: Mid-November to mid-April

**Hours of Operation**: 9 a.m. - 3:30 p.m.

| 1990/91 Prices | Full Day | Half Day |
|---|---|---|
| Adult (19-54) | $30 | $25 |
| Youth (13-18) | $25 | $20 |
| Child (6-12) | $15 | $11 |
| Young at Heart (55+) | $15 | $11 |

up with the 7-11 Ski Heaven Ski School and be entertained and taught while mom and dad enjoy the freedom to ski at their own pace.

For the rest of the skiing population though, Tod is a challenging mountain that offers a variety of runs. Intermediates and advanced intermediates enjoy the lion's share of the terrain, with numerous top to bottom runs that will test skill and endurance. The bulk of the runs are found off the Shuswap Chair on long, sweeping runs such as Cruiser and Blazer. Tod has improved its grooming quite a bit in the last few years with the addition of new specialized equipment and better-trained staff.

The dominant feature of the hill is the above treeline dome which offers steep, short pitches off to the right and more gradual, open areas off to the left. Many people ride the Crystal Chair almost exclusively to access this area and the powder snow it receives. While you're exploring, try out the hidden run Challenger in the middle of the mountain accessible from Upper Shortcut over to Crystal Chair.

Even though Tod receives 680 cm (22 ft.) of snow, one thing to know is that a stretch of sunny weather in the spring time is sure to melt down the exposed Burfield side of the mountain faster than the Shuswap side. Even when the Burfield chair is closed due to lack of snow, there is often good skiing from the Shuswap chair. It's a good idea to phone ahead if you're thinking of coming in late March or April.

A problem at Tod has been the lack of on-hill accommodation. The new 45-room hotel at the Burfield base is the first step to providing a ski in, ski out chalet experience. Remember also that many of the motels in Kamloops offer special skier packages. An infrastructure for more development recently went into place at the ski hill base, including the first residential subdivision, which sold out quickly in the 1988-89 ski season.

Keep an eye on Tod because even though it's been around for thirty years, the sleeping giant is just starting to stretch itself.

# Cat Skiing

*Snow cats are used for hill grooming, but they also take skiers to untouched powder.*

Your breath fogs the window of the warm snowcat as you lean closer to gaze at the laden evergreens. Large clumps of snow silently break free and the branches swing upward in their sudden weightlessness. Looking ahead, there is no visible trail through the forest as the snowcat confidently winds its way up through the deep untracked powder, untracked powder that you will soon be skiing. Your pulse accelerates as you think of the vast expanse of deep powder waiting for just you and this select group.

Snowcat skiing is gaining the recognition it deserves, not just as a lower-cost alternative to heli-skiing but for the equally enjoyable experience it provides. There are also advantages to cat skiing that are to be considered. While helicopters can be grounded by inclement weather, snowcats can operate almost all of the time. Although you will not accumulate as much vertical as a heli-skier, it's less hurried so that no one need feel intimidated.

Cat skiing has been happening in the Kootenays since 1975 and has been gaining a larger following each year. If you're looking for a deep-powder ski vacation without the crowds of the ski hills or the expense of heli-skiing, a cat skiing experience is a great choice.

# SELKIRK WILDERNESS SKIING

Allan and Brenda Drury                                      (604) 366-4424
Meadow Creek, B.C.
V0G 1N0

Selkirk Wilderness Skiing caters to small groups on a five-day, six-night basis, accommodating them in the Meadow Mountain Lodge. The 9000-square-foot lodge has room for 24 guests and features spacious living and recreation rooms, fireplaces, sauna and an open-air jacuzzi.

Transportation to the peaks of Meadow Mountain is in a warm, twelve-passenger snowcat. The snowcat rides are 15 to 30 minutes long depending on the length of the runs. A variety of slopes covering 20 square miles of terrain can be skiied, and most groups ski an average of eight runs a day for a total of 12,000 to 16,000 vertical feet.

Fly to Castlegar and an airport bus will take you to Nelson where you will be met and transported to Meadow Creek, 1 1/2 hours north of Nelson on Highway 31. Car pools are often arranged, call for information.

**1989/90 Prices\*:**
Low Season  $1,395
Middle Season  $1,600
High Season  $1,830

*\*5 days skiing/6 nights accommodation/all meals*

# LEMON CREEK LODGE

Box 68                                                      (604)355-2403
Slocan, B.C.
V0G 2C0

Located 64 km northwest of Nelson in the beautiful Slocan Valley, Lemon Creek Lodge is the newest operation running a snowcat for skiers. They are offering two- and four-day packages for up to twelve people.

Relax in the sauna or hot tub after the day and enjoy cosy cabins and good food in the restaurant. Lemon Creek Lodge also has conference and meeting facilities if your company would like to combine business and powder.

# CAT POWDER SKIING

Box 1479                                            (604)837-9489 (collect)
Revelstoke, B.C.
V0E 2S0

The upper reaches of Mt. MacKenzie are put to good use by Cat Powder Skiing. While the bottom third of the mountain may be serviced by lifts, it's the top, with an average of 1,500 cm (50 ft.) of snow per year, where the great powder skiing takes place. A heated snowcat takes about 65 minutes in the morning to get up to the right elevation but after that the rides are only 15 to 30 minutes depending on the length of the runs.

The season runs from December to mid-April. There are 65 different runs, from bowls to trees, and can be 500 m to 2,000 m long.

Skiers can book two-, three- and five-day packages which include unlimited vertical each day, professional guide service, local transportation, accommodation in Revelstoke and all meals.

**1989/90 Prices\*:**
  Low Season  $1,000
  High Season  $1,175

*\*5 days including all meals, accommodation, skiing*

# GREAT NORTHERN SNOW-CAT SKIING

Box 220, Station G                                  (403)287-2267
Calgary, Alberta,
T3A 2G2

Great Northern is based in Trout Lake, B.C., only 75 km southeast of Revelstoke, in the heart of the Selkirk Mountains. Three-day and six-day packages are available.

A new lodge was built just outside Trout Lake in 1990 to accommodate 14 to 18 people. Future expansion is planned. Meals are served family style around a large dining table, and the word is out that the cook is great. She's a dedicated lady who puts up jams and preserves in the summer to tempt the guests in the winter after a long day of skiing powder.

For the best conditions, the season runs from early December to late April. The valley bottom averages 850 cm (28 ft.) of snowfall annually with more at higher elevations. Normal temperatures range from -12°C to -6°C.

**1989/90 Prices\*:**
  Low Season  $1,615
  High Season  $2,315

*\*6 days skiing, all meals, accommodation*

# Heli Skiing

*Canadian Mountain Holidays offers heli-skiing in eight different mountain areas.*

Heli-skiing is the ultimate skiing experience. The endless expanse of virgin powder, crystalline blue skies and knife-edged mountain ridges slicing the horizon are every skier's dream. The reality is better.

"Thwok thwok thwok." Rotors slap the air as clouds of snow whip your face. Your eyes water. The guide motions everyone down and you huddle together while the chopper lands. The door swings open, and the group piles in, quickly picking a seat and clicking into seatbelts. These thin straps may be the only thing holding the skiers down as they fidget and strain toward the windows for a view of the approaching mountain tops. You can feel the excitement leap as the guide points at a ridge with the white velvet carpet spread out for you and the select few in this helicopter. The moment you've been waiting for all year is here.

Many people are addicted to heli-skiing simply because it's the most exhilarating experience a powder skier can have. The incredible terrain and virgin powder, the excitement of the helicopter flights and the camaraderie of the groups turn the simple act of skiing into nirvana. It's no wonder that most heli-ski businesses have a very high rate of return among their guests. Once you tasted heli-skiing, you'll always crave it.

Some first-time heli-skiers experience a certain amount of intimidation. Relax. Everyone is there to have a good time, but like many activities, there are a few things to keep in mind.

Ken Hardy and Doug O'Mara of Whistler Heli-Skiing recommend some rules of conduct. They stress "safety first" for everyone involved, and the best way to achieve that is to always listen to the guide. You endanger not only yourself but the other members of the party if you don't follow instructions. As for your ability, you don't need to be an expert skier, but to enjoy heli-skiing, you should be at least an intermediate skier and in good physical condition. Groups are broken up into ability levels and the guides are willing to help with powder techniques.

Now for the fun part — the skiing! Don't let your excitement overwhelm your common sense though. Enjoy the adrenalin rush, but pay attention to the guide and your surroundings.

The guide's main duty is to bring everyone home. So when you're skiing:

- Don't ski past the guide
- Stop when he stops
- Stay close to the guide's tracks and
- Have fun!

### Helicopter Safety

1. Keep your head down. No need to explain why.
2. Drag your skis on the snow around the helicopter.
3. Never approach the machine on skis.
4. The safest spot is next to the helicopter, within the pilot's range of vision. If a gust of wind does cause the rotors to dip down, you're in close and out of the way.
5. Keep your seatbelt done up until the guide is out and has set the guide pack on the snow. He will ask you to gather around and hang on to it until the helicopter has lifted off. This way the pilot and guide know everyone's location.
6. Never go near the the tail of the helicopter.

# WHISTLER HELI-SKIING

Box 368                                          (604)932-4105
Whistler, B.C.
V0N 1B0

Whistler Heli-Skiing has over 100 licensed runs on glaciers near Whistler. They ski on Brandywine, Rainbow and Ipsoot Mountains and on the Spearhead Glacier. On low visibility days, they descend to ski the trees on Rainbow Mountain. The heli-ski season is from November to May but the best conditions are between February and March. The day includes the heli-guide, gourmet mountain-top lunch, transportation to the heli-pad and and an apres-ski party.

Clients are required to prebook at least the day before. All clients must be 19 years old.

# CANADA HELI-SPORTS INC.

P.O. Box 460                                     (604)932-2070
Whistler, B.C.                                   (604)932-3512
V0N 1B0

Pilot Jim Logue has been flying in the Whistler area for many years. His heli-ski license covers an area north-west of Whistler beyond Ipsoot Mountain and bordered on the north by the Pemberton Valley. Some of these mountains are so remote they don't even have names. Canada Heli-Sports takes up no more than 10 in a group, offers a gourmet mountaintop lunch and transportation to and from their heliport.

# TYAX HELI-SKIING

Box 849                                          (604)932-7007
Whistler, B.C.                                   U.S. Toll Free: 1-8800-663-8126
V0N 1B0

Tyax Heli-Skiing is affiliated with Tyax Mountain Lake.

The resort 100 km (60 miles) north of Whistler in Gold Bridge. They offer daily trips from Whistler Resort, and three- and seven-day packages from Tyax Lodge. Reservations for day trips can be made at The Mountain Shop in the Delta Mountain Inn, between 3 p.m. and 6 p.m. the afternoon before.

Tyax has two major heli-ski areas, each with more than two dozen runs: the Spearhead Range, east of Blackcomb Mountain and the Powder Mountain area, southwest of Whistler.

# KOOTENAY HELICOPTER SKIING LTD.

Box 717                                    (604)256-3121
Nakusp, B.C.                               1-800-663-0100
V0G 1R0

Skiers are flown into the world-famous Selkirk and Monashee Mountains around Nakusp for deep powder runs of up to 5,000 vertical feet.
Kootenay can accommodate up to 45 skiers each day, divided into groups
with their own personal guide. A relaxing soak in Nakusp Hot Springs
finishes the day and then back to the Kuskanax Lodge for the night.

# NELSON HELI-SKIING/ K.M.B. TOURS

Box 867                                    (604)354-4371
Nelson, B.C.
V1L 6A5

A short flight takes the skiers to the vicinity of Kokanee Glacier Park in
the Selkirk Mountains. Daily heli-skiing and three day packages are
available. Accommodation is at a new 40-person lodge near Lardeau,
north of Kaslo on Kootenay Lake.

# SELKIRK TANGIERS HELICOPTER SKIING

Box 1409                                   (604)344-5016
Golden, B.C.                    Operations: (604)837-5378
V0A 1H0

Revelstoke is the access point for Selkirk Tangiers to fly their skiers into
the Selkirk Mountains. Their base of operation is the Best Western Way-
side Inn on Hwy 1 at Revelstoke. Selkirk Tangiers also has a small office
in the Alpine Village Mall.

The Selkirk Lodge in the Albert Icefield (see Ski Touring section) is
part of the Selkirk Tangiers operation. They provide helicopter access
from Revelstoke for package ski touring trips.

The Albert Canyon Heli-Plex is located at the border of Glacier National Park between Rogers Pass and Revelstoke. This new base offers
easy access to the Albert Ice Fields and to incredible ski runs in the
Tangiers River Valley. There are over 200 runs in the operation's 3,000
square kilometres of skiable terrain.

# R.K. HELI-SKI PANORAMA

Box 695
Invermere, B.C.
V0A 1K0
(604)342-6494
(604)342-3889 (winters)
Banff (winter only): (403)762-3771
Reservations: 1-800-528-1234

*Powder abounds in the Purcell Mountains.*

R.K. Heli-Ski specializes in programs for the first-time heli-skier and those who wish to ski at a "no pressure" pace. The skiing takes place in the southern Purcell Mountains and the area encompasses over 2,000 square kilometres and offers 120 runs varying in length from 500 (1,600 ft.) to 2,000 (,6500 ft.) vertical metres.

The Hal Bavin Heli-Plex is located at Panorama Resort near Invermere. A daily escorted charter bus, not included in package price, departs the Banff Springs Hotel at 7 a.m. and downtown hotels at 7:30 a.m. and returns at approximately 7 p.m.

# MIKE WIEGELE HELICOPTER SKIING

Box 249                             (403)762-5548
Banff, Alberta          U.S. Toll Free 1-800-661-9170
T0L 0C0

Mike Wiegele has been taking heli-skiers into the Cariboo and Monashee ranges for twenty years. Based in Blue River, B.C., an escorted bus will meet skiers at the Kamloops airport at the beginning of the ski week. The Mike Wiegele Heli Village Resort provides comfortable accommodation and great food. Many skiers are repeat customers and book their vacations a year ahead, so don't leave it to the last minute.

Mike Wiegele's operation is known and respected world-wide, and has been the site of several ski movies, including some of Warren Miller's films. It's also the home of the World Powder 8 Championships.

# CANADIAN MOUNTAIN HOLIDAYS

Box 1660          (403)762-4531
Banff, Alberta    (604)273-9100
T0L 0C0           or 1-800-663-2515

This is the other big name in Canadian heli-skiing. CMH operates out of eight different areas: the Gothics, the Bugaboos, the Bobbie Burns, the Cariboos, the Monashees, Revelstoke, Valemount and Galena out of Trout Lake. Their guides are well trained and experienced on local terrain.

Seven-day packages and intro weeks for first time heli-skiers are available, with return transportation from the Calgary Airport. Accommodation is provided in comfortable, mountain lodges serving excellent food in a casual and fun atmosphere.

*Canadian Mountain Holidays.*

# COAST MOUNTAIN HELI-SKI CENTRE

c/o Chilko Lake Holdings, Ltd.          (604)398-8828
Box 4750
Williams Lake, B.C.
V2G 2V7

The Chilko Lake Lodge is base camp for Coast Mountain Heli Ski. The Lodge is a luxurious log building at an elevation of 4,000 ft. which means great skiing is just outside the door. Gold medalist skier Rosi Mittermaier selected tbe Coast Mountain runs, and qualified ski guides lead the way.

Weather permitting, you will enjoy 100,000 vertical feet of skiing during the week. The routes are changed every day for fresh powder. In the evening, relax with the Chilko Lake Lodge's outdoor whirlpool, heated indoor pool or sauna.

# PURCELL HELICOPTER SKIING

Box 1530                                              (604)344-5410
Golden, B.C.
V0A 1H0

A five-minute flight takes skiers to Purcell Helicopter's area of over 2,000 square kilometres. Their skiable terrain is south and west of Golden and north of the Bugaboos.

They offer three-, five- and seven-day heli-skiing packages as well as daily heli-skiing. Packages include all meals, accommodation at the Golden Rim Motor Inn, deep powder lesson, guide service and guaranteed minimum ski footage.

Try a Heli-Tely/Cross Country skiing adventure package. A helicopter will fly you up to a remote alpine meadow for the day and then fly you back down.

# GREAT CANADIAN HELI-SKIING

Box 1050                                              (604)348-2361
Golden, B.C.
V0A 1H0

Another heli-ski operation in the Purcell and Selkirk Mountains area attests to the abundance of great skiing in the area.

Five-, six- and seven-day packages are available with return transportation from the Calgary Airport (for groups only). Accommodation is at the Best Western Glacier Park Lodge in the Rogers Pass area.

# Nordic Skiing

*Cross-country skiing at Kimberley.*

Cross country skiing can be a relaxing tour along track-set trails or a rugged backcountry ski touring adventure. All are part of the Ski B.C. experience. Most of the downhill areas in B.C. offer nordic trails to complement their alpine facilities and many of those trails have been mentioned in the section on that particular resort. The following are the trails and touring areas that are independent of ski hills.

## SOUTHWESTERN B. C.

Known for its abundance of downhill areas, the southwest also offers excellent nordic facilities.

# BENNO'S COUNTRY ADVENTURE TOURS

1958 West 4th Ave.      (604)738-5105
Vancouver, B.C.,
V6J 1M5

Benno's Country has been operating cross country adventure tours since 1974. They feature small group numbers, experienced guides and transportation to the sites in their mini-buses. The tours visit selected resorts and are offered in one day packages as well as Weekend Getaways and Ski Marathons. Special tours are arranged at Christmas, New Year's and Easter. For all levels of ability.

# GARIBALDI PROVINCIAL PARK

Ministry of Parks, South Coast Region      (604)929-1291
1610 Mount Seymour Road
North Vancouver, B.C.
V7G 1L3

The Diamond Head area in Garibaldi Park just north of Squamish offers some challenging back country touring. Book the hut at Elfin Lakes through the local Parks Branch office in Brackendale (604)898-3678.

# HOLLYBURN RIDGE CROSS-COUNTRY

Snow Phone: (604)925-2704
Rentals & Ski School: (604)922-0825

The Hollyburn Ridge Ski Centre is on the road up to Cypress Bowl in West Vancouver. It caters to all abilities. They have kilometres of groomed trails on twenty three different runs cut through the towering trees overlooking Vancouver. There is a good beginner's loop lit for night skiing and two warming huts on the trails. There is also a tobaganing hill below the parking lot and ski centre.

# LOST LAKE NORDIC TRAILS

Resort Municipality     (604)932-5535
of Whistler
Box 35
Whistler, B.C.
V0N 1B0
Vancouver:(604) 688-6018

Whistler Resort is best known for its downhill skiing at Whistler and Blackcomb Mountains. It also is home to 15 kilometres of groomed trails around Lost Lake Park only 3 kilometres from the village. A warming hut is located on the shores of Lost Lake.

The Valley trail offers another 10 km of marked-only tracks and trails criss-cross the golf course.

*Cross-country adventure awaits.*

# MAD RIVER NORDIC

Box 284     (604)932-3188
Whistler, B.C.
V0N 1B0

An adventurous nordic experience is available with Mad River Nordic in the Callaghan Valley 16 km south of Whistler. They have 60 km of groomed trails at elevations ranging from 800 m (2,400 ft.) to 1,375 m (4,124 ft.). There are warming huts along the trails.

# MT. STEELE

B.C. Forest Service                                      (604)485-9831
7077 Duncan Street
Powell River, B.C.
V8A 1W1

Back country trails and cabins have been developed by Gibson's Tetrahedron Ski Club with the assistance of the Forest Service. The trails are signed and marked.

# CARIBOO/CHILCOTIN

The light, dry snow of the Cariboo Chilcotin is perfect for cross country skiing. Each winter, numerous marathons and loppets are attended by skiers from across the province and the north western U.S. who are drawn by the excellent snow conditions. As a result, the variety of trails and terrain for nordic skiing in the region are the most extensive in B.C. The heart of cross country skiing in the Cariboo is the village of 100 Mile House which has earned the title of "International Nordic Ski Capital" because of the concentration of activities and facilities.

# 100 MILE NORDIC SKI SOCIETY

Box 1888                                         (604)791-5552
100 Mile House, B.C.
V0K 2E0

The Cariboo Marathon is in its second decade as Western Canada's largest event and attracts up to 1,500 skiers in early February. It is included in the provincial and C.S.A.'s National Ski Odyssey loppet circuit.

*Nordic enthusiasts often venture off the groomed tracks to make new discoveries.*

# 108 GOLF & COUNTRY INN

Comp. 2, RR #1, 108 Ranch      (604)791-5211
100 Mile House, B.C.      1-800-452-5233
V0K 2E0

A perrenial favourite of Cariboo visitors, this full service resort on 230 hectares (575 acres), has a heated pool, fine dining, kitchenettes, and access to 200 km cross country ski trails. Six kilometres of the golf course are lit for night skiing.

# ALPINE WILDERNESS ADVENTURES

General Delivery      (604)372-2338
Tatlayoko Lake, B.C.      H492430 Chilanko JJ Channel-Ranch
V0L 1W0

Warm up in the cosy log cabins after wilderness adventures, photo safaris and cross country skiing with Alpine Wilderness Adventures.

# BIG BAR GUEST RANCH

Box 27, Jesmond      (604)459-2333
Clinton, B.C.
V0K 1K0

The ranch has full service accommodation, a licensed dining room, hot tub, cross country skiing.

# CARIBOO WEST OUTFITTERS LTD.

Box 4208      H426546 YR, Nechako Channel
Gary & Peggy Zorn
Quesnel, B.C.
V2J 3J3

This is a complete outfitting/guide service for trail rides, fishing trips, and cross country skiing.

# CHILKO LAKE LODGE

Box 4750      (604)398-8828
Williams Lake, B.C.
V2G 2V7
N678596 Chilanko JJ Channel

A beautiful log lodge offering complete packages, with cross country skiing, snowmobiling, mountaineering skiing, sleigh rides and ice fishing. This is the home of the Coast Mountain Heli Ski Centre.

# COHO FISHING ADVENTURES

104 East 49th Avenue     (604)324-8214
Vancouver, B.C.
V5W 2G2
U.S. Toll free 1-800-663-8755

Coho Lodge is located at Sheridan Lake, 480 km (300 miles) northeast of Vancouver at an elevation of 1100 m (3600 feet) above sea level. The lodge provides all modern comforts with kilometres of trails around the lake.

# CROOKED LAKE RESORT

Box 389
Williams Lake Radio H69-2824
100 Mile House, B.C.
(604)395-7128
V0K 2E0

*Gorgeous scenery on B.C.'s nordic trails.*

Crooked Lake Resort offers cabins, a restaurant and a convenience store. They have cross country trails and snowmobiles are welcome.

# EAGLE LAKE RESORT

General Delivery                          JJ Channel N424757, P.G. Operator
Tatla Lake, B.C.
V0L 1V0

At Eagle Lake Resort you'll find cabins, cross country skiing, skating, snowshoeing and snowmobiling.

# GUNNER'S CYCLE

C 230-108 RR#1                                       (604)791-6212
100 Mile House, B.C.
V0K 2E0

Across from 108 Resort, Gunner's Cycle has cross country ski sales, rentals, lessons and tours with a complete line of equipment, clothing and accessories.

# HILL'S HEALTH & GUEST RANCH

C26, 108 Ranch, RR#1
100 Mile House, B.C.
V0K 2E0

Hill's Ranch offers cross country ski and weight loss vacations. It has luxurious accommodations, a licensed restaurant, swimming pool, two jacuzzis, two saunas, an aerobic studio and 200 km of cross country trails.

# NATURE HILLS RESORT

C.215, Johnstone Road, RR#1          (604)593-4659
Lone Butte, B.C.
V0K 1X0

Cabins, a restaurant and cooking facilities are available at this resort. Twenty kilometres of groomed trails and 10 km of ski skating lanes are maintained. Ski rentals, repair and instruction are also offered.

# RED COACH INN

Box 760          (604)395-2266
100 Mile House, B.C.          1-800-663-8422 (Canada)
V0K 2E0

Famous as the headquarters of the Cariboo Marathon, this hospitable inn offers cross country ski packages, 48 rooms and suites, licensed dining room, sauna, and whirlpool. Red Coach Inn trails are linked to the 99 Mile Nordic Centre which is developed to International Racing Federation Standards and contains 30 km of competitive track. A 2.5 km loop is lit for night skiing.

# TEN-EE-AH LODGE

Box 157          N-692024 on JS channel. Peter or Ulli Uogler
Lac La Hache, B.C.
V0K 1T0

The Ten-ee-ah Lodge is open year round with log cabins, a licensed restaurant, set cross country ski tracks, and sled dog tours.

# TYAX MOUNTAIN LAKE RESORT

General Delivery     (604)238-2221
Gold Bridge, B.C.
V0T 1P0

Tyax is the largest log structure on the west coast offering 28 comfortable suites, a dining room, bar, lounge, fitness centre and heli-skiing as well as 30 km of groomed cross country trails that circle Tyaughton Lake and beyond.

# THE WELLS HOTEL & GALLERY

Box 134
(604)994-3427
Wells, B.C.
V0K 2R0

*Spruce Lake area in Cariboo-Chilcotin.*

This facility offers programs and arts events for the entire family, a restaurant, handicrafts, 25 km of groomed trails and 50 km of marked cross-country trails. It has equipment rentals and is an excellent telemarking area.

# WHITEHORSE LAKE GUEST RANCH

Box 31                                         (604)396-4192
Lac La Hache, B.C.
V0K 1T0

The Whitehorse Lake Guest Ranch is a year round resort offering cottages with private bath and kitchen, cross country skiing and downhill skiing nearby.

# VANCOUVER ISLAND

The upper elevations of the Island receive an enormous amount of snow each winter as the Pacific storms crash against its coastline. Even as Victoria holds its annual flower count in the middle of winter, Island residents are also enjoying the many cross country skiing opportunities available.

## MT. CAIN ALPINE PARK SOCIETY

Box 1225                                     (604)956-3849
Port McNeill, B.C.
V0N 2R0

The Island's newest nordic ski area by Woss on the Nimpkish River offers 20 km (12 miles) of unmarked trails, a day lodge and ski rentals.

*Groups, as well as individuals and families, are welcome at these nordic resorts.*

# MT. WASHINGTON

Box 3069                                         (604)338-1386
Courtenay, B.C.                          Snow Report: (604)338-1515
V9N 5N3

A major downhill area, it also offers 30 km (19 miles) of triple trackset trails at an elevation of 1,450 m (3400 ft.). The Battleship Lake, Helen Mackenzie trails and Paradise Meadows plus the West Meadow's hills for experts provide a nordic setting for all skiers.

Nearby Strathcona Park offers an extensive touring trail network.

# OKANAGAN-SIMILKAMEEN

The Okanagan has extensive nordic trails with the added feature of being at high elevations. These ski areas receive an abundance of snow and a wealth of the famous Okanagan sunshine.

## APEX MOUNTAIN GUEST RANCH

Box 426      (604)492-2454
Penticton, B.C.
V2A 6K6

Located 22 km (14 miles) along the road to Apex Alpine, this full facility guest ranch offers 48 km of groomed trails and 9 km of ski skating lanes. The trails are between the 900 m (3,000 ft.) and 2100 m (7,000 ft.) level.

## IDABEL LAKE RESORT

Ste 13D, C-2, RR#5      (604)762-1339
Kelowna, B.C.
V1X 4K4

The lodge is located 50 km from Kelowna on Hwy 33 and is 20 minutes from Big White. Lakeside, gothic-arch cabins have kitchens, lofts and can accommodate up to eight people. Linen (including pillows) is not supplied. A small restaurant is in the main lodge. Idabel ski club offers 34 kilometres of well-groomed cross country trails in the area.

## POSTILL LAKE LODGE

Box 854      (604)860-1655
Kelowna, B.C.
V1Y 7P5

These trails, at the 1,400 m (4,600 ft.) level, were developed by the Forest Service and the Postill Recreation Society. The lodge has 60 km of groomed trails, ski rentals, and RV hookups. It is located 14 km (9 miles) north of Kelowna and is open year round. There are snowshoeing and back-country skiing opportunities, also.

# KOOTENAY COUNTRY

The Kootenays are famous for deep champagne powder and casual lifestyles. There is excellent alpine touring in Kokanee Glacier Park and cross country trails at Nancy Greene Lake, Kokanee Creek and Stagleap Provincial Parks. The parks are within a one hour radius of Nelson and all have daylodges.

## LEMON CREEK LODGE

Box 68                                                        (604)355-2403
Slocan, B.C.
V0G 2C0

Spectacular mountain scenery awaits you on the 10 km (6 miles) of cross country trails at Lemon Creek Lodge. Explore the alpine on telemark skis. Two and four day cat skiing packages for up to twelve people are available.

## WHITEWATER INN

Box 532                                                       (604)352-9150
Nelson, B.C.
V1L 5R3

This cosy bed and breakfast is located 10 km south of Nelson on the way to Whitewater ski area. Thirty kilometres of groomed and 15 km of ski skating trails are maintained.

Nelson's Nordic Club has 45 km (27 miles) of their own trails near the city.

Paulson Trails: 20 km northeast of Castlegar near Nancy Greene Lake are 40 km of trails.

Providence Lake Trails: Near Phoenix Mountain west of Grand Forks. There are 30 km of nordic trails around the lake and on the old mining roads.

Black Jack Cross Country Ski Club: Located across the highway from Red Mountain in Rossland, the club has excellent facilities including a daylodge, lessons, ski shop, repairs and rentals, daycare, warming huts and 40 km (25 miles) of marked and groomed trails.

# B. C. ROCKIES

These mountains are home to five heli-skiing companies, a variety of downhill resorts and extensive cross country ski trails. The long valley of the Rocky Mountain Trench provides wonderful panoramas and easy access to these areas.

## BEAVERFOOT LODGE

Box 1560           (604)346-3205
Golden, B.C.        (604)346-3216
V0A 1H0

Bring your own skis and tour the 60 km of groomed trails along the headwaters of the Kootenay and Kicking Horse River drainage. Beaverfoot Lodge is a large log building amid giant spruce trees offering comfortable rooms, sauna and home cooking.

## EMERALD LAKE LODGE

Box 10             (604)343-6321
Field, B.C.
V0A 1G0
Toll Free (reservations) 1-800-663-6336

This luxury resort is located 8 km (5 miles) north of Field and offers 85 rooms and 24 cabins, all with private fireplaces and balconies. The lodge offers ski rentals, ski shop, instruction and repairs to complement its 25 km of groomed trails. Near Lake Louise ski area.

# LAKE O'HARA LODGE

Box 1677                                                           (604)343-6418
Banff, Alberta
T0L 0C0
Winter Reservations (403)762-2118

Spell-binding scenery, powder snow and a luxurious lodge combine to create a special vacation. The lodge, open year round, is located in Yoho National Park and offers 11 km of groomed trails and 11 km of ski skating lanes. There is no vehicle access in winter and guests ski in from the highway on an easy 12 km (7 miles) packed trail to the lodge.

# SNAKE RIDGE TOURING

Box 1029                                                           (604)423-4033
Fernie, B.C.
V0B 1M0

Vince and Mary Shier are both Cansi Certified Telemark Instructors and offer private and group lessons along with weekend clinics at Snow Valley ski area. The Snake Ridge Touring Guest House provides cozy, private accommodation minutes from the hill.

# TOP OF THE WORLD GUEST RANCH

Box 29                                                             (604)426-6306
Fort Steele, B.C.
V0B 1N0

At the foot of the spectacular Steeples range near Cranbrook, the ranch is open year round and offers fun family vacations. Nordic guests have 50 km of trails to ski or may book guided alpine ski-tours.

# HIGH COUNTRY

A broad and diverse region, stretching across the middle of British Columbia, High Country offers all types of skiing for all types of skiers. The Rogers Pass and vicinity are the centre for heliskiing and touring while downhill and cross country ski facilities are scattered throughout the towering mountains of the region.

*Beginners can find lots of trails.*

## CORBETT LAKE COUNTRY INN

Box 327       (604)378-4334
Merritt, B.C.
V0K 2B0

The rolling grasslands south of Merritt are the site of 34 km of trails at Corbett Lake. Open from December to February, the inn offers ski rentals, accommodation with cooking facilities and a restaurant.

## HELMCKEN FALLS LODGE

Wells Gray Provincial Park   (604)674-3657
Box 239
Clearwater, B.C.

Located at the entrance to Wells Gray Provincial Park, the Helmcken Falls Lodge has 50 km (30 miles) of groomed trails and 200 km (125 miles) of backcountry skiing. Ski rentals and instruction are available.

# LOGAN LAKE

Copper Valley Motor Inn     (604)523-9433
Logan Lake Hotel     (604)523-6211

Only minutes off the Coquihalla Highway are 22 km of track set trails at Logan Lake. There are no trail fees but there are donation boxes at the trail head. The area is only 20 minutes from Tunkwa Lake, Walloper Lake and Lac Le Jeune Ski area.

# MOUNTAINEER INN

Box 217     (604)566-4477
Valemount, B.C.     Toll Free: 1-800-663-4462
V0E 2Z0

Snowmobiling is a specialty of this resort but they also have 20 km of groomed trails, ski rentals, instruction and repair. Ski packages are available.

# SALMON ARM MOTOR HOTEL

Box 909     (604)832-2129
Salmon Arm, B.C.     Toll Free (B.C. & Alberta reservations) 1-800-663-5308
V1E 4P1

# SHUSWAP INN

Box 1540, Trans Canada Highway West     (604)832-7081
Salmon Arm, B.C.
V1E 4P6

# TWIN ISLAND RESORT

Box 7     (604)838-7587
Salmon Arm, B.C.
V1E 4N2

The previous three lodgings offer a ski bus service for their guests to LARCH HILLS cross country area. The ski complex contains 150 km (94 miles) of trails at 1,000 to 1,200 m in elevation. The local ski club grooms and sets 60 km of track. They also host the Canadian Ski Odyssey's 40 km (25 mile) Reino Keski-Salmi Loppet in January. Larch Hills is 25 minutes from Salmon Arm. Twin Island Resort has some trails and offers ski packages to Larch Hills.

# WALLOPER LAKE RESORT

Box 1095                                                    (604)372-9843
Kamloops, B.C.
V2C 6H2

Located on the Coquihalla Highway, the Walloper Lake Resort is only 4 km from Lac La Jeune and also from the Stake Lake's 50 km trails system. Cabins with cooking facilities are available and the resort has 15 km of its own trails.

# Ski Touring

*Telemark skiing is a popular form of touring.*

British Columbia offers endless expanses of untouched alpine wilderness waiting patiently for ski touring adventurers. Huts and cabins dot the glaciers and plateaus of B.C.'s mountain ranges and are generally available for public use. The peace and solitude of trekking through the high mountains, relying completely on yourself and your partners, and enjoying the beauty and the effort of the tour are deeply satisfying.

Throughout the province, the provincial and national parks have excellent facilities for winter mountaineering and touring. For more information, the British Columbia Road Map and Parks Guide provides a listing of parks and facilities or contact the Information Unit, B.C. Parks, 4000 Seymour Place, Victoria, B.C., V8V 1X5; (604)387-3940.

Many people aren't fully equipped to explore the winter alpine on their own but still yearn for the backcountry experience. A number of companies have been set up to assist others in their explorations and provide the knowledge to do it safely. These outfits are often operated by experienced people who want to share their love of the mountains with you.

## SOUTHWESTERN B. C.

### SEA TO SKY TOURS

Office: 1311 W. 1st Street
North Vancouver, B.C.
Mailing Address:
1928 Nelson Avenue
West Vancouver, B.C.
V7V 2P4
(604)984-2224

## OKANAGAN-SIMILKAMEEN

### DEE LAKE LODGE

#71, 3535 Casorso Road
Kelowna, B.C.
V1Y 2V6
(604)861-4617
Radio Phone: Vernon JP N693243

### HEADWATERS CROSS-COUNTRY

Box 350
Peachland, B.C.
V0H 1X0
(604)767-2400

## KOOTENAYS

### MOUNTAIN HIGH RECREATION

Box 128
Slocan, B.C.
V0G 2C0
(604)226-7790
(604)355-2518

### VALHALLA MOUNTAIN TOURING

Box 284
New Denver, B.C.
V0G 1S0
(604)358-7714

## HIGH COUNTRY

### ANSTEY SAFARIS

Box 3038
Salmon Arm, B.C.
V1E 2T0
(604)832-6811

### MONASHEE CHALET

Interior Alpine Recreation
Box 132
Blue River, B.C.
V0E 1J0

### BEST WESTERN GLACIER PARK LODGE

Glacier National Park
Rogers Pass, B.C.
V0E 2S0
(604)837-2126

### SELKIRK MOUNTAIN EXPERIENCE

Box 2998
Revelstoke, B.C.
V0E 2S0
(604)837-2381

### BLANKET GLACIER CHALET

c/o Nordic Ski Institute
Box 1050
Canmore, Alberta
T0L 0M0
(403)678-4102

### ERICK SUCHOVS

Box 2188
Revelstoke, B.C.
V0E 2S0
(604)837-3682

*Touring can take you to great areas of untouched snow.*

## BRITISH COLUMBIA ROCKIES

### ADVENTURE BOUND CANADA

Box 811
Golden, B.C.
V0A 1H0
(604)344-2639

### DIANA LAKE LODGE

Box 2397
Banff, Alberta
T0L 0C0
(403)762-4396

### GOLDEN ALPINE HOLIDAYS

Box 1050
Golden, B.C.
V0A 1H0
(604)348-2361

### ISLAND LAKE LODGE

Box 580
Fernie, B.C.
V0B 1M0
(604)423-3700

### MOUNT ASSINIBOINE LODGE

"The Matterhorn of the Rockies"
Box 1527
Canmore, Alberta
T0L 0M0
(403)678-2883

### NORTHERN LIGHTS ALPINE RECREATION

Box 399
Invermere, B.C.
V0A 1K0
(604)342-6042

### PINNACLE MEADOWS/ MISTAYA ALPINE TOURS

Box 990
Golden, B.C.
V0A 1H0
(604)344-6689

### PTARMIGAN TOURS

Box 11
Kimberley, B.C.
V1A 2Y5
(604)422-3270

### SELKIRK LODGE

Box 1409
Golden, B.C.
V0A 1H0
(604)344-5016

*Alpine touring is also popular in B.C.*

## CARIBOO CHILCOTIN-COAST

### ALPINE WILDERNESS ADVENTURES

Tatlayoko Lake P.O., B.C.
V0L 1W0
(604)372-2338

### HIDDEN MOUNTAIN SKI TOURS

c/o Sam Whitehead
Kleena Kleene, B.C.
V0L 1M0
Radio Phone: Kleena Kleene 3G

### SPRUCE LAKE TOURS

2375 W. 35th Avenue
Vancouver, B.C.
V6M 1J7
(604)263-2118
(604)238-2425

### WHITE SADDLE AIR SERVICES

Box 22
Tatla Lake, B.C.
V0L 1V0
Radio Phone: Prince George H699698

*Touring allows skiers to reach areas not accessed by ski tows or nordic tracks.*

## ABOUT THE AUTHOR

Heather Doughty was among the flood of Ontario immigrants to Whistler, B.C., in November of 1982. She figured that with her resort management diploma in hand, she'd have no problem finding a job and having some fun for a ski season before moving one to bigger and better things — the "real world." That was nine years ago, and she hasn't found anything better or more "real" than living in Whistler, skiing, windsurfing and mountain biking with her new family of friends.

After working in numerous restaurants at night so she could ske, and travelling in Europe and Southeast Asia, Heather entered a unique and challenging writing program at Selkirk College in 1988. Her goal was to blend creativity, sport, travelling and earning a living. Even her choice of school was influenced by the fact that Whitewater and Red Mountain — homes of incredible powder skiing — were in the area.

Heather's goal was realized in the winter of 1990, when she spent six weeks visiting and skiing the resorts of British Columbia in preperation for writing Ski B.C. It was a tough job, but somebody had to do it!

She married her partner in the project and best friend, Victor Beresford in August 1990.

# PHOTO CREDITS

# Other books From Lone Pine Publishing

## SKIING IN ONTARIO
*by Gary Horner*
An insider's guide to alpine skiing in Ontario. Includes an extensive
beginner's guide to buying equipment.
$12.95 softcover    256 pp.    5 1/2 x 8 1/2    ISBN 0-919433-93-6

## CANADIAN ROCKIES BICYCLING GUIDE
*by John Dodd and Gail Helgason*
Over 60 tours, covering the mountains of Alberta, British Columbia
and northwest Montana.
$9.95 softcover    256 pp.    5 1/2 x 8 1/2    ISBN 0-919433-09-X

## CANADIAN ROCKIES ACCESS GUIDE
*by John Dodd and Gail Helgason*
The essential guide for exploring the rockies by car, on horseback, or
on foot. There are 115 day hikes included. Third Edition.
$12.95 softcover    256 pp.    5 1/2 x 8 1/2    ISBN 0-919433-92-8

## THE LONE PINE PICNIC GUIDE
## TO BRITISH COLUMBIA
*by Nancy Gibson and John Whittaker*
Explore B.C. on over 50 perfect picnics, from the coast to the
mountains. Includes local history, menus, places of interest and more.
$11.95 softcover    264 pp.    5 1/2 x 8 1/2    ISBN 0-919433-60-X

## BRITISH COLUMBIA WILDLIFE VIEWING GUIDE
*Principal author: Bill Wareham*
Explore 67 of B.C.'s finest wildlife viewing sites. Also included is a list
of the 50 most sought after wildlife species and where to find them.
$8.95 softcover    96 pp.    5 1/2 x 8 1/2    ISBN 1-55105-000-5
$14.95 hardcover    96 pp.    5 1/2 x 8 1/2    ISBN 1-55105-001-3

## YUKON CHALLENGE
*by John Firth*
The story of the men and dogs of the 1,600-kilometre Yukon Quest,
one of the world's toughest dogsled races.
$12.95 softcover    240 pp.    5 1/2 x 8 1/2    ISBN 0-919433-85-5

---

Look for these books at your local bookstore.
If they're unavailable, order direct from:

*Lone Pine Publishing*
#206, 10426-81 Avenue,
Edmonton, Alberta T6E 1X5
Phone (403) 433-9333
In Vancouver: (604) 687-5555